American McGee's™

ALICE™

Prima's Official Strategy Guide
Greg Kramer

The Prima Games logo is a trademark of Prima Communications, Inc. Prima Publishing® is a registered trademark of Prima Communications, Inc., registered in the U.S. Patent and Trademark Office.

Senior Project Editor: Brooke N. Hall
Product Manager: Jennifer Crotteau
Editorial Assistant: Michelle Pritchard

ISBN: 7615-2979-9
Library of Congress Catalog Card Number: 00-10924
Printed in the United States of America

00 01 02 03 BB 10 9 8 7 6 5 4 3 2 1

Dedication

To Adam "Ba" Kramer, King of All Wild Things.

Acknowledgments

Thanks to all those who usually appear on this page. You're getting too numerous to mention but I love you all.

For performing like the well-oiled machine we've become, thanks to the Prima team of Jennifer, Brooke, and Michelle P. Thanks also for the care and vision, respectively, of Cinamon Vann and Robin Berni.

For his tireless support and frank advice, thanks most of all to American McGee's Alice producer, R.J. Berg. Thanks also to product manager Jonathan Harris, and Justin Holst, from the product testing team.

Prima Games
A Division of Prima
Communications, Inc.

3000 Lava Ridge Court
Roseville, CA 95661
(916) 787-7000
www.primagames.com

Table of Contents

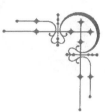

Introduction

When I first heard that someone was going to make an action game out of Lewis Carroll's classic tales, *Alice's Adventures in Wonderland* and *Through the Looking Glass and What Alice Found There*, I thought, "Why?" It seemed like an odd choice as the basis for a fast-paced and typically gory action game.

Then I thought about it some more. Why wouldn't you want to make a game out of those books? With their bizarre characters and twisted landscapes, such a game would be a culmination of where computer gaming was already headed, not to mention one hell of a mind trip.

And who better than the self-styled renegade designer American McGee to make it all happen?

It's clear that his path is one of vision and overflowing creativity.

With its superlative level design, vivid characters, exhilarating puzzles, and horrifically beautiful aesthetic (an elegant mating of *The Nightmare Before Christmas* and Edward Gorey's artwork), *American McGee's Alice* is the most singular and memorable game experience in years.

Structure of this Guide

This strategy guide is intended to serve players of all levels and provide easy reference for players desiring only a little boost rather than an explicit spoiler.

Whenever possible, the guide avoids overlapping with the Install Guide that shipped with the game. In some instances, however, it's necessary to reiterate important points. The walkthrough was written based on the Normal difficulty level.

To help you through Wonderland, this guide is structured as follows:

♣ Chapter 1: A full discussion of all basic gameplay elements including moving, fighting, jumping, swimming, rope swinging, and more.

♣ Chapter 2: A comprehensive directory of all Toys and power-ups.

♣ Chapter 3: An exhaustive gallery of the characters who inhabit Wonderland: friends, foes, bosses, and non-combatants. Enemy descriptions include methods of attack, weaknesses, and tactics for defeating them. Bosses are briefly outlined here, and are discussed fully in the appropriate walkthrough chapters.

♣ Chapters 4–12: The walkthrough chapters cover every region and level of Wonderland. These chapters describe how to navigate every map, defeat every puzzle, and claim every Toy. The walkthroughs also contain enemy lists and detailed tactics for defeating every boss, including the Queen herself.

♣ Appendix A: An interview with American McGee.

part 1
Gameplay Overview

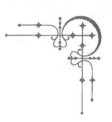

Chapter 1

Alice in Wonderland— Basic Training

The Wonderland of *American McGee's Alice* is meant to be an unfamiliar, disorienting place. Still, that's no reason to wander around confused and lost. This chapter introduces you to all the things you will be doing on land, in water, and in the air.

Skill Levels

Easy

Medium

Hard

Nightmare

Choose your skill level but be sure you know what you're getting into.

The first choice you must make is the skill level at which you'll play: Easy, Medium, Hard, or Nightmare. Several variables are affected by this choice:

1. The amount of damage done by Alice's attacks

2. The amount of damage enemies do to Alice

3. The difficulty of environmental challenges

Choosing Easy, for example, makes Alice's attacks very powerful and reduces the amount of damage done when enemies strike. Higher levels progressively reverse these states. Alice's attacks aren't as effective, because her enemies are relatively stronger and they inflict more damage.

Tip

IF YOU'RE A GAMING NOVICE, BUT WANT TO EXPERIENCE THE RICH AND UPROARIOUS WORLD OF AMERICAN McGEE'S ALICE WITHOUT THE CHALLENGES AND FRUSTRATIONS OF FULL-BLOWN GAMEPLAY, SELECT EASY. YOU STILL HAVE TO LEARN TO MOVE AND FIGHT, BUT DOING SO WON'T REQUIRE AS MUCH SKILL.

IF, ON THE OTHER HAND, YOU WANT TO IMMERSE YOURSELF IN THE DYNAMIC AND MIND-BENDING TWISTS AND TURNS OF THE FULL GAME, SET DIFFICULTY ON AT *LEAST* MEDIUM. MASOCHISTS CAN, OF COURSE, ENJOY THE HORRIFIC CHAOS AND CHALLENGE OF NIGHTMARE.

Interface

The American McGee's Alice *interface*

The interface in *American McGee's Alice* is designed to be as unobtrusive as possible. Its most basic elements are discussed in the game's Install Guide. Items deserving extra discussion, however, are covered in this section.

Meters

There are two meters with which you should be concerned: Sanity and Strength of Will.

Sanity

The red meter on the left represents Sanity. Essentially, Sanity represents Alice's "health." If she loses her Sanity, nothing can save her (except, of course, reloading a saved game). When Alice takes damage (in combat or by falling excessive distances), her level of Sanity decreases.

Sanity can be restored in two ways:

1. Alice can absorb Meta-Essence Crystals, the life force of everything in Wonderland. The larger the crystal, the more Meta-Essence it contains. Meta-Essence restores *both* Sanity and Strength of Will in equal amounts. For more information on Meta-Essence, see Chapter 2.

2. Alice can also collect Sanity Shards. These squat, red crystals can be found strewn about all over Wonderland. Grabbing one immediately restores a finite amount of Sanity.

Meta-Essence Crystals

Sanity Shards

Strength of Will

The blue meter on the right represents Strength of Will. In conventional gaming parlance, Strength of Will is basically ammunition for your Toys.

The Ice Wand devours Strength of Will as it sprays cold death.

Different Toys consume Strength of Will at different rates. Flinging Cards, for example, uses only a small amount of Strength of Will. Firing a shot from the Blunderbuss, however, can eat up your entire supply. Some Toys (like the Ice Wand) consume Strength of Will continuously as long as you hold the attack button.

Once Alice has drained her Strength of Will, she can no longer use most of her Toys until some Will is restored. In this state, she can only use or throw the Vorpal Blade or swing the Croquet Mallet, which require no Strength of Will.

Strength of Will is restored in three ways.

1. As with Sanity, Strength of Will is restored by absorbing Meta-Essence. See earlier discussion on Sanity and Chapter 2 for more details.

2. Alice gets an instantaneous increase in Strength of Will by finding Vials of Will. These blue tubes contain a fluid that restores a finite amount of Alice's Strength of Will.

3. At Easy and Medium skill levels (only) Strength of Will recharges gradually over time.

Vial of Will

Toy and Power-Up Indicators

Alice is currently using the Cards (see lower left) and is under the influence of the Rage Box power-up (see lower right).

The Toy you're currently armed with is shown in the lower-left corner of the screen.

If you've picked up certain power-ups, like the Rage Box, or the Dead Time Watch, the power-up's symbol appears in the lower right corner while the power-up is active. The indicator retracts as the power-up's influence is expended, eventually disappearing as it expires.

See Chapter 2 for more information on Toys and power-ups.

Indicators

There are two types of targeting aids you can activate at your discretion.

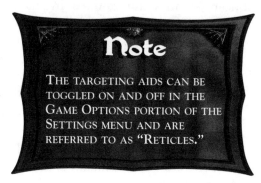

Note

THE TARGETING AIDS CAN BE TOGGLED ON AND OFF IN THE GAME OPTIONS PORTION OF THE SETTINGS MENU AND ARE REFERRED TO AS "RETICLES."

Target Indicator

When activated, the Target indicator displays where an attack will land. It appears in two forms:

1. A ring of blue light: If you've armed a Toy that tracks its target, the ring of light appears around the nearest enemy in the direction Alice is facing. This "target lock" tells the Toy to do its best to find that enemy, even if he moves from his or her current position. The Toy's accuracy depends on how well it tracks and how skillfully the enemy moves. A target lock doesn't guarantee a hit.

2. A blue dot: If no enemies are in view, are too far away, or if you've armed a Toy that doesn't track its target, the Target indicator appears as a single blue dot. Pressing the attack button sends the attack toward the location of the dot until it strikes something.

The Target indicator encircles its victim with a ring of blue. Fire away!

Jump Indicator

The Jump indicator appears as a pair of feet on the ground and allows you to see where Alice will land if she jumps.

Note

THE JUMP INDICATOR ONLY APPEARS WHEN ALICE IS STANDING STILL; IT ISN'T USED FOR RUNNING JUMPS.

The Jump indicator shows where Alice will land if you press the Jump button. Move the indicator by adjusting the height and angle of your view with the mouse.

The Jump indicator is useful for simple, standing jumps, but isn't very helpful for jumps at moving targets. The indicator may be disabled from the Settings menu.

See "Jumping" later in this chapter for more information on using this indicator.

Basic Movement

Though fighting and leaping are central to the *American McGee's Alice* experience, most of your time is spent simply moving about.

American McGee's Alice's navigation system should be familiar to anyone with third-person action game experience, and it's easily customizable for players with their own preferred control set-up.

For novices, even if you've never played an action game before, it shouldn't take long to get the hang of controlling Alice.

Novice Advice: Movement Theory

The controls in *American McGee's Alice* are based on a simple division of labor: One hand (your mouse hand) controls which direction Alice faces, the other controls what she does.

Use the mouse to turn Alice right and left as you run, walk, and jump. The direction Alice is facing is very important when jumping and fighting. If, for example, you move the mouse so that Alice is looking down, she will target her attack in that direction, too.

If Alice is looking down, she'll attack in that direction. The angle of the game's "camera" also indicates how far Alice will take a standing jump.

The ideal set-up (for a right-handed player) is one that puts all basic keyboard functions in your left hand and mouse control in your right. This control set-up is outlined in the following section.

Control Set-Up: A Suggestion

You may find this set-up for *American McGee's Alice* as easy to use as the game's default controls. It is based on a commonly-used set-up for several popular action games.

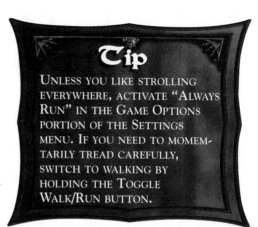

Tip

UNLESS YOU LIKE STROLLING EVERYWHERE, ACTIVATE "ALWAYS RUN" IN THE GAME OPTIONS PORTION OF THE SETTINGS MENU. IF YOU NEED TO MOMEM-TARILY TREAD CAREFULLY, SWITCH TO WALKING BY HOLDING THE TOGGLE WALK/RUN BUTTON.

- ♣ Primary Attack: Left Mouse Button

- ♣ Alternate Attack: Right Mouse Button

- ♣ Move Forward: E / I

- ♣ Move Backward: D / K

- ♣ Jump/Swim Up: A / ;

- ♣ Climb/Swim Down: Z / /

- ♣ Turn Left: S / J

- ♣ Turn Right: F / L

- ♣ Strafe (Sidestep) Left: W / U

- ♣ Strafe (Sidestep) Right: R / O

- ♣ Toggle Walk/Run: Shift / Shift

- ♣ Use/Push/Climb: Spacebar / Spacebar

- ♣ Summon Cheshire Cat: H / C

- ♣ Cycle through Toys: + and - or Third/Fourth Mouse Button or Mouse Wheel

> ### Note
> THE FOLLOWING KEY ASSIGNMENTS ARE LISTED WITH THE SETTING FOR RIGHT-HANDED PLAYERS FIRST, FOLLOWED BY THE ASSIGNMENT FOR LEFT-HANDED PLAYERS.

If you find this awkward or discover assignments that work better for you, change them. The ultimate goal is to make the controls second nature. If, after several hours, you still have to think about which button to push, consider tinkering with the control assignments.

Fighting

You must fight effectively if you want to have any hope of saving Wonderland. Even if you're playing on the Easy skill level, there are certain techniques you must master. These skills are very easy to attain and nicely challenging to master.

Combat is one of the most important parts of the game, but not the only part.

Defense

Before discussing attacking, there are a few things you must know to avoid the "slings and arrows" (and battle axes) of others.

♣ When under attack, stay in constant motion. A stationary target is very easy to hit.

♣ Use natural cover to protect yourself from projectile attacks. Duck behind bookshelves, rocks, or any other environmental object that you can put between you and the oncoming attack.

♣ Jump over low attacks.

♣ Back away from jab attacks.

♣ Don't be afraid to run if you're over matched. If you need to collect your self and pick the right weapon, it's better to do so in a safe place rather than just standing and bleeding.

Take cover to avoid damage.

Hand-to-Hand Combat

Some Toys (Vorpal Blade, Mallet, and Ice Wand) are "melee" weapons. They can be used in close hand-to-hand combat.

Unfortunately, this type of fighting puts you right in your enemy's attack range (unless he or she is using a shorter weapon than you are).

Standing still is certain death even against dullards like this Club Card Guard.

> # Note
>
> ALL WEAPONS, EXCEPT THE DEMON DICE AND BLUNDERBUSS, HAVE TWO MODES OF ATTACK: PRIMARY AND ALTERNATE.

It's sheer suicide to stand in front of an enemy and stab away while he or she hacks you to pieces.

Instead, bob and weave. In other words, stay in constant motion and attack quickly. This approach has two benefits:

1. A moving target is hard to strike. You'll take less damage.
2. Quick strikes are hard to defend against. Wait for an opening, inflict your damage, then back away. Though it's tempting to keep attacking after you've found an opportunity, most foes will eventually counterattack. It's best to be out of range when they do.

The key to constant motion is the strafe; frequently bob backward and forward, but most of your motion should be lateral. The main reason for this: getting behind your opponent.

Keep moving—strafe to make yourself hard to hit.

Most (not all) enemies are vulnerable from the rear. They can't attack targets behind them and require some time to turn around to face you. During this interval, get in some good licks. Rear attacks can be as effective as frontal assaults.

Note

STUDY THE ATTRIBUTES OF EACH OF THESE MELEE TOYS (SEE CHAPTER 2) TO UNDERSTAND THE SPECIFIC TACTICS TO USE WITH EACH.

Projectile Combat

Most combat involves projectiles fired from medium-to-long range.

Several Toys (Vorpal Blade, Cards, Mallet, Eyestaff, and Blunderbuss) can

Tip

AFTER YOU'VE MASTERED MOVING WHILE YOU FIGHT, YOU NEED TO WORK ON A MORE ADVANCED SKILL: CIRCLE STRAFING.

THOUGH LESS IMPORTANT THAN IN MORE COMBAT-ORIENTED GAMES, THE CIRCLE STRAFE WILL SERVE YOU WELL IN AMERICAN McGEE'S ALICE.

THE BASIC IDEA OF THE CIRCLE STRAFE IS TO AVOID YOUR ENEMY'S ATTACK WHILE CONSTANTLY UNLEASHING YOUR OWN.

WHEN FIGHTING, STRAFE IN EITHER DIRECTION. AS YOU DO, ADJUSTING YOUR MOUSE SO YOUR TARGET IS ALWAYS IN FRONT OF YOU. IF YOUR FOE STANDS STILL AND YOU KEEP HIM IN THE CENTER OF YOUR VIEW, YOU'LL NATURALLY TRAVEL IN A LARGE CIRCLE AROUND HIM. IF YOU DO THIS FAST ENOUGH, YOU CAN GET BEHIND ENEMIES VERY EASILY.

AFTER YOU MASTER THE CIRCLE STRAFE, TRY RANDOMLY CHANGING DIRECTION TO MAKE YOURSELF HARDER TO HIT.

fire projectiles in either primary or alternate modes. The Mallet, for example, can be swung as a club (primary attack) or used to launch a deadly croquet ball (alternate attack). The Cards, on the other hand, can *only* be used as projectile attacks in both modes.

Firing from a distance is a good tactic, but there are some exceptions.

Projectile attacks aren't always the safest way to fight.

♣ Most projectile attacks are hard to land. Even tracking shots (ones that will try to follow a moving target) don't always hit their target. You can waste considerable Strength of Will without damaging your foe.

♣ Some weapons (such as the Blunderbuss) require you to stand still while you fire, which makes you vulnerable to attack.

♣ Use cover to shield yourself from projectile counterattacks. Duck behind nearby objects to protect yourself.

♣ Keep an eye on your Strength of Will (blue meter on the right). When it runs out, you're only able to use your Vorpal Blade or the Mallet, if you have it, until you replenish the supply.

Using the Blunderbuss makes you a very easy target when it primes to fire.

Untargeted Combat

Some Toys (Demon Dice, Jackbomb, Jacks, and Eyestaff) don't really target enemies. You can dictate where they go by the direction Alice is facing and (for the Dice and Jackbomb) the angle of the camera, but they don't really deal with individual targets like other Toys.

Toss Toys like the Jackbomb toward enemies and they'll create some kind of havoc. Use the angle of your view to control how far you throw them.

The key to using these weapons effectively is placement, angle, and timing.

♣ Throw these Toys in the general direction of enemies. Take cover while the Toys wreak havoc. After you've got some experience, use attacks like these as a distraction to allow Alice to pass unscathed.

♣ The angle of Alice's view dictates how far away a Demon Dice or Jackbomb attack will land. Just below horizontal is maximum distance, staring straight down is minimal.

♣ The conventional target indicator doesn't appear when you use these weapons.

♣ Learn how much time it takes to use these attacks and how long they take to detonate once thrown. Target the attack in front of a moving enemy so it'll detonate as he or she arrives—knowing how long a Toy takes to detonate is essential to your success.

Jumping

Next to combat, the most frequent move Alice uses is jumping on, over, or to various things. Skillful jumping is crucial.

Learning to jump is just as important as learning to walk.

Standing Jumps

Jumping from a standing position is the simplest kind of jump. There are two types of standing jumps.

Short Jumps

Short jumps can be accomplished without a running lead. Learn to use your mouse to affect the distance of your leap.

The Jump indicator (a pair of feet) appears when you move the mouse downward, just past horizontal (looking at the ground). When the Jump indicator first appears, it is very far away from Alice. If you press Jump, she jumps to the location of the Jump indicator.

The Jump indicator first appears when your view reaches this angle ...

... continuing to move the mouse downward brings the target closer to Alice's current position.

Adjust the location and distance of the Jump indicator by moving the mouse up, down, or sideways.

When you have the indicator in the desired location, jump. Alice makes a crisp simple jump to that location.

Alice will jump to the location of the feet, without fail.

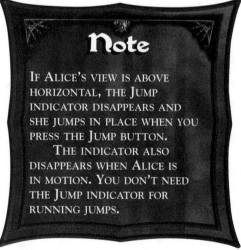

Note

IF ALICE'S VIEW IS ABOVE HORIZONTAL, THE JUMP INDICATOR DISAPPEARS AND SHE JUMPS IN PLACE WHEN YOU PRESS THE JUMP BUTTON.

THE INDICATOR ALSO DISAPPEARS WHEN ALICE IS IN MOTION. YOU DON'T NEED THE JUMP INDICATOR FOR RUNNING JUMPS.

Climbing Jumps

When Alice needs to jump up to a high ledge, position her just below and in front of the ledge. Make sure she's looking up toward her destination and press Jump. She automatically jumps and grabs hold of the ledge above her.

While looking straight up, press Jump and Alice will hop to get a grip on ledges over her head.

Finally, press the Forward key to make Alice pull herself up onto the ledge. If it's too narrow for Alice to stand on, pressing Forward has no effect and she remains hanging by her fingers.

Move Alice laterally along a ledge by pressing the Strafe keys.

Then press the Forward key to pull up.

Running Jumps

Many jumps are so long that Alice must get a running start.

Some jumps require a running start.

To take a good running leap, first find the shortest distance to jump. For example, if a plank extends further into an abyss than the rest of the floor, make sure Alice uses this extra solid ground to extend her jumping range.

Once Alice is pointed in the right direction, move the view so that you're looking down on her. Start running.

Look down on Alice when doing running jumps. This lets you take off at the last possible instant.

When you see her reach the end of solid ground, press Jump.

If you don't quite make the jump, Alice often grabs hold of the target ledge by her fingertips. Press Forward to pull up to safety.

Ropes

Many obstacles require climbing or swinging on ropes.

Ropes and vines are everywhere, but you must know how to use them.

Grabbing

To grab a rope, jump toward it. Alice automatically grabs hold.

Climbing

Once on a rope, you can climb up or down. To go up, press the Use key. To shimmy down, press the Down key.

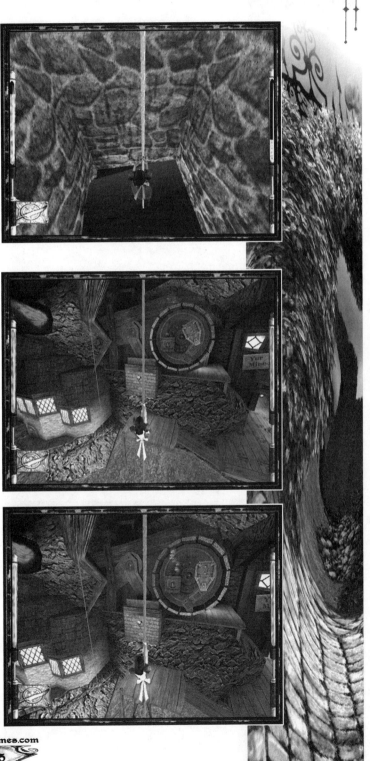

*Adjust your position on a rope by
pressing Use or Down.*

Swinging

Using ropes in *American McGee's Alice* is
very realistic.

After you're on a rope, make it swing
in the desired direction by pressing
Forward. Pressing Forward repeatedly at
the right time helps you gain momentum
and swing in increasingly long arcs.
Pressing the Backward key while she's
swinging backward also increases her
momentum. Swinging in long arcs allows
you to jump very long distances.

*To start swinging, face the direction
you want to go
and press and hold Forward.*

*When Alice starts to swing backward,
release Forward.*

*When she starts to swing forward again,
hold the Forward key to gain
even more momentum.*

Just as in real life, this is a cumulative process. Holding Forward makes Alice extend her legs. When she reaches the apex of her forward swing, release the Forward key and let her swing backward. As she starts to come forward again, press the Forward key and she stretches her legs out to gain added momentum and swing even farther forward.

Remember, where you are on a rope affects how far you can jump. If you're near the top of the rope, the swing arc is always very short, giving you very little forward momentum to make long jumps. If you're near the bottom of a rope, you can use the rope's maximum swing arc.

Dismounting

Dismount a rope at any time by pressing the Jump button. If you're swinging, the

momentum of the swing causes Alice to dismount in the direction of the swing. If, on the other hand, you press Jump while the rope isn't swinging, Alice simply drops straight down.

*Press Jump to release Alice's grip
on the rope and jump in the direction
the momentum carries her.*

Swimming

Alice can swim if the situation calls for it, but she can't stay in, let alone under, the water for long … on her own.

Breathing

Help arrives in the form of the Mock Turtle. This strange beast grants Alice a tool that allows her spend long stretches of time under water: the Mock Turtle Shell.

The Turtle Shell works by holding a stock of air from which Alice can breathe. Whenever Alice submerges, she automatically holds the shell (it appears translucent) over her back and head.

Alice meets the Mock Turtle in the Pool of Tears level. Later he gives Alice the power to stay underwater for long periods of time.

The Turtle Shell appears translucent over Alice's head. It holds a limited supply of air that must be replenished periodically.

The stock of air, however, doesn't last forever. Alice must either surface or find an underwater air source to refill the shell. Underwater sources are easily identified: Look for bubbles.

If you see bubbles flowing underwater, stop for a moment to refill your shell, then continue swimming.

Look for flows of bubbles to refill the Turtle Shell.

Moving Underwater

Your controls function underwater almost the same as on land, but not quite.

Forward, Backward, Strafe Left, and Strafe Right all function the same but are relative to the direction Alice is facing. If she's facing the surface, Forward causes her to swim toward the surface. If she's facing the bottom, Forward takes her there.

Up and Down are, however, not relative. Up causes her to surface no matter what position she's in, and Down causes her to sink.

If Alice is facing the bottom, pushing Forward causes her to swim in that direction.

Floating

Several puzzles in the game require Alice to use steam vents to move otherwise impossible distances. The air rising from the vent inflates Alice's skirts and allows her to float and climb on the pillar of air.

When you have Alice floating on air, view her from above to keep her in the flow of steam.

The trick to using these vents effectively is to keep Alice from drifting out of a vent's column too soon. To do so, always adjust the camera to look down on Alice (by moving the mouse down). From this angle, you can make the adjustments necessary to keep Alice centered in the steam flows and, when necessary, direct her onto another column of steam or onto solid ground.

Chapter 2

Alice's Toy Box

In the downside up world of Wonderland, Toys are weapons. The more fun it is, the more deadly. Most of Alice's Toys have two different modes of attack and all are a blast.

Consult this directory for descriptions of all of Alice's Toys and Wonderland's essential power-ups.

Toys

Vorpal Blade

The Vorpal Blade is Alice's most basic toy. Its warped but razor-sharp blade is the mainstay of her attack arsenal. Just because it's the first Toy she receives, however, doesn't mean it's weak.

The Vorpal Blade's primary attack is a basic but brutal slash. It's sharp and strong enough to decapitate or halve an opponent. The direction of the slash depends on which direction Alice is moving and the angle in which she is looking.

In secondary mode, Alice can throw the Vorpal Blade as a projectile attack. It doesn't, however, track its target, instead flying straight to the location of the Target indicator when the attack was launched. To use this attack effectively, either launch it at stationary targets or learn to lead and anticipate targets. The latter skill takes time to acquire but learning it pays off.

Neither Vorpal Blade attack consumes any Strength of Will—it is the only projectile weapon with no Strength of Will cost.

Cards

These playing Cards are all wild and deadly. Both attacks are projectiles, but with very different effects.

In primary mode, Alice can fling the cards one by one. These projectiles move quickly and track moderately well. Individually, they don't consume much Strength of Will but, over the course of a fight, they add up considerably. They're your fastest-firing projectiles.

In alternate mode, Alice can throw the Cards "52-Pick-Up" style as a group. This cloud of Cards seeks out the targeted victim, and all strike at once. The multi-card attack tracks better than the individual cards but sports a very high Strength of Will cost.

Croquet Mallet

The Croquet Mallet is the best clobbering weapon and boasts a very sound projectile attack. Still, its speed limits its effectiveness in certain situations.

The Mallet's primary attack is a melee one. Alice swings the heavy Mallet according to the direction in which she's moving and the angle of the view. Victims of this attack also receive a residual electrical shock from the magically enhanced Toy. This attack *requires no Strength of Will*.

Alternately, the Mallet can be used as a projectile weapon with Alice's limitless supply of croquet balls. She tosses them into the air, smacking them golf-style at the targeted enemy. If the ball doesn't find a target, it'll bounce off the first solid (non-flesh) surface it strikes. Alternate mode consumes a small amount of Strength of Will.

In both modes, the Mallet is, relative to other Toys, slow. Start your attack early and time it to strike exactly when you want it to.

Demon Dice

The Demon Dice are awesomely powerful weapons, summoning evil minions to do your dirty work. They come, however, with a big price tag.

Demon Dice have only one mode of attack. Use the special target indicator (a golden pentagram) to indicate where you want to throw the Demon Dice. Angle the view to move the indicator away from Alice and press the attack button to launch. Remember this: Demon Dice need a lot of room to open up and spawn. In a confined space, their effect is unpredictable.

Demon Dice are the only cumulative Toy; the more you find, the more powerful the weapon becomes. One Die summons the lightning-spewing Lesser Demon. Two Demon Dice can summon the tail-whipping, fire-lobbing Serpent Demon. Three Demon Dice can summon the gigantic ice-spewing Demon Lord. The Strength of Will cost increases with each resulting Demon. Which Demon you get with multiple Demon Dice is random.

If, for some reason, the Demon Dice are unable to do their job (if one falls off a platform), they vaporize and the Strength of Will you spent will be restored.

Jackbomb

The Jackbomb is an explosive device that amuses as it destroys. This maniacal jack-in-the-box's primary attack is a timed explosion. Like the Demon Dice, the Jackbomb is thrown to locations, not at targets. Unlike the Demon Dice, however, there's no special target indicator. Aim the Jackbomb with the angle of your view as you would a jump; just below horizontal is the farthest throw, looking straight down is the shortest. When the fuse is spent, the Jackbomb detonates in a devastating explosion, shredding any enemy in its blast radius. Make sure Alice is out of harm's way because the Jackbomb can do considerable damage. Each bomb uses a moderate amount of Strength of Will.

In alternate mode, the Jackbomb is a rotating flamethrower. As it lands, the Jack pops up and begins to spray flame in a fast-moving circle. Victims are set ablaze for several seconds after being ignited. This attack costs considerable Strength of Will.

Ice Wand

Your visit to the ice caverns of Wonderland yield this chilly toy. Use it wisely.

In primary attack mode, the Ice Wand shoots a continuous spray of freezing ice as long as you hold the Attack button. Enemies find it difficult to attack while being sprayed and freeze as they expire. The Ice Wand doesn't specifically target but can injure multiple enemies at once. Beware that this weapon devours Strength of Will at an alarming rate.

The Ice Wand's alternate attack erects a wall of ice in front of Alice. This protective shield lasts for a finite time and finally melts away. It costs relatively little to build. The construction process, however, leaves Alice vulnerable until the shield is built. You may build multiple ice walls at a time.

Jacks

Jacks may not seem like impressive offensive weapons, but they certainly are. One toss can cut down a Jabberspawn before it can even attack.

The primary mode for the Jacks is a random toss. The Jacks bounce frantically, striking any enemy they happen to hit. They will fix on a target after they make contact, and seek out enemies. After a finite amount of time, the Jacks return to Alice's hand. The cost for this powerful attack is minimal.

Alternate mode allows you to throw a handful of Jacks that doggedly pursue a selected target. When they track down their prey, all the Jacks converge at once and hit their target until it expires. This power, however, comes with a high Strength of Will price tag.

Jabberwock Eyestaff

The Eyestaff is a potent mystical Toy assembled from the very eye of the mighty Jabberwock.

The primary attack mode, like the Ice Wand, is a cumulative attack. Hold the Attack button until the Eyestaff charges (you can move while this happens). Continue to hold the button and the staff shoots a beam of pure energy. The longer you hold the button, the more Strength of Will it consumes. When you release the Attack button, the staff finishes jolting with a punishing charge.

The staff's alternate mode is positively awe inspiring. Hold the alternate Attack button for the duration of the Eyestaff's considerable charging time. After it's fully charged, the staff sends several flares skyward. These flares damage anything overhead. Almost immediately, the flares fall to earth, landing in jarring fiery crashes. These flares can injure you, so stand still as the attack develops. You can release the Attack button anytime, but fewer flares will be launched. The massive time required for this attack leaves you very vulnerable, so don't use it when you're under active attack.

Blunderbuss

The Blunderbuss may look like a simple musket, but it isn't.

This Toy has only one mode of fire, but it's a doozy. One shot from this gun is an impossibly massive explosive charge that knocks Alice on her rump, shakes the ground, and liquidates any living thing in its blast radius. Don't use this gun if you're near a ledge, you can fall off.

So awesome is the Blunderbuss that one shot requires your entire supply of Strength of Will.

Power-Ups

Meta-Essence

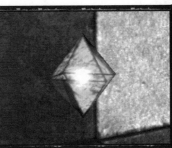

Meta-Essence is the life force of all things in Wonderland. Consuming it replenishes Alice's Sanity and Strength of Will in equal amounts.

Meta-Essence can be found two ways: strewn about the landscape or escaping from a recently slain creature.

It also comes in four sizes: small (pyramidal), medium (octahedral), large (heart-shaped), and super. The larger the crystal, the more Sanity and Strength of Will it replenishes.

Larger Meta-Essence Crystals from dead enemies gradually deteriorate as they're exposed to air, growing smaller as time passes. Crystals found in the environment don't decay.

Sanity Shard

Sanity Shards replenish Alice's Sanity when consumed. They come in two types and are found throughout Wonderland.

Vial of Will

The Vial of Will increases your Strength of Will when consumed. The Vials come in two varieties and are hidden throughout Wonderland.

Rage Box

The Rage Box empowers Alice with a fearsome temper. Beyond the obvious physical transformation, the Rage Box has two effects. Alice's attack power is increased while her vulnerability to damage is decreased. Unfortunately, it lasts only a limited time.

Grasshopper Tea

Grasshopper Tea allows Alice to run faster and jump higher. Plus, it makes for a cool get-up. The effects of this fragrant, insectoid tea last only a short time.

Mock Turtle Shell

The Mock Turtle Shell enables Alice to stay underwater for extended periods of time. Not indefinitely, mind you, but far longer than without it. The Mock Turtle Shell holds a limited amount of air from which Alice can breathe. To refresh this supply, you must either surface or find an underwater bubble supply. Pause briefly over the bubbles and you can continue swimming.

You acquire this power-up from the Mock Turtle in the beginning of the Wonderland Woods. It activates automatically, thereafter, whenever Alice submerges in water.

Dead Time Watch

The Dead Time Watch can stop time, but only for a short duration. It is reusable and has a five-minute recharge time. Stopped time freezes enemies in place but also prohibits changing the status of any part of the environment (such as opening doors).

Darkened Looking Glass

The Darkened Looking Glass grants the power of invisibility for a brief time. While the Darkened Looking Glass is in effect, Alice may move about and even attack without fear of retaliation. Watch for "blinking." It means you're about to become vulnerable.

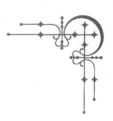

Chapter 3

Wonderland Residents

Wonderland has always been known for its unique inhabitants. Under the influence of American McGee and Rogue Entertainment, however, they've become positively vivid.

Other than Alice herself, there are four types of characters you'll encounter: standard enemies, bosses, friends, and non-combatants.

Our Heroine: Alice

Once a carefree, clever, imaginative youth, Alice has become a scarred and hardened teenager. The fire that killed her entire family left her silent and disturbed.

Awakened by the White Rabbit, Alice is intense and dangerous, wielding an array of deadly Toys. As she spends more time in Wonderland, her skill with Toys is likely to increase, enhancing the speed of her attacks. Enemies that take considerable effort to destroy in early levels may become easier targets later.

Enemies—Standard

The Queen's foot soldiers are numerous and deadly. The key to victory lies in understanding each enemy's attack style and vulnerabilities.

Club Card Guard

Club Card Guards lack versatility, but shouldn't be taken lightly. Their spear jab is quick but can be easily dodged by retreating or sidestepping. The more challenging spear swing is harder to avoid—sidestep away from the swing.

Use the Club Card Guard's attacks against him. He's extremely vulnerable after the spear swing—after he misses, dive in and strike. Get behind the Club Card Guard; he's slow to turn around and very vulnerable from the rear.

Diamond Card Guard

The Diamond Card Guard's spear has a spinning blade, making him much more dangerous than the Club Card Guard. His favorite move is a brutal combo: an uppercut stab followed by a spin and slash. The Diamond Card Guard hurls diamond-shaped projectiles from a distance, which don't track as well as your Cards, making them easy to avoid.

Like the Club Card Guard, the Diamond Card Guard is vulnerable when his attacks miss—get behind him and hack away.

Boojum

The Boojum is a flying nightmare. It swoops in and lets loose a deafening shriek that punctures eardrums and shoves its victim backwards. Boojums lurk near high ledges, waiting to startle and kill unsuspecting climbers. One well-timed scream can send even the most sure-footed climber over the precipice.

The best defense against the Boojum scream is constant motion. If you can get out of the scream's kill zone, you'll escape the brunt of the attack.

Whenever possible, attack Boojums from a distance. This keeps you out of scream range and away from their teeth. Cards and the Mallet's alternate attack work quite well against them. When in close combat, stick to the fast-striking Blade.

Army Ant Soldier

These lowly Ant grunts carry standard-issue muskets with bayonet attachments. Their long-range attack is a potent but slow-moving musket shot. Though the shots are easy to avoid, the Ants can reload quickly.

Close combat is where these Ants shine. First, they use their razor sharp pincers in a variety of attacks. Second, if you stand still too long they'll stab you with their bayonets and toss you into the air.

Attack Ant Soldiers from a distance with Mallet shots or any other ranged weapon. After they're sufficiently damaged, they'll retreat—take the opportunity to send a croquet ball right up the old thorax.

Army Ant Commander

Ant officers are even tougher than their underlings. Instead of a firearm, they carry a finely sharpened cutlass and a pack full of grenades. They don't mind getting physical, either, with a bone-jarring punch and a pincer squeeze.

Keep your distance and stay on the move. The fast-moving grenades have a considerable blast radius. Getting in close is effective but you'll pay a price if you're caught standing still.

Blood Rose

You probably won't notice a Blood Rose until it sprouts to its towering size and begins hurling giant thorns at you. These projectiles move fairly fast and come in large clusters. Better to duck behind something than try to dodge each thorn. Up close, the Rose slashes with its ragged leaves.

Ranged attacks are your only option. Take single shots as you peek out from behind barriers. The Blood Rose is rooted to the ground, so it can't pursue or adjust position for a better shot.

Evil Mushroom

These innocent-looking fungi spring to life when you get too close, immediately sucking you into their jaws. The result is a devastating and agonizing grind in the Mushroom's row of long teeth. After it finally spits you out, retreat to avoid repeating this horrible process. But as you flee, you'll get a face-full of poisonous spore gas. This cloud moves with alarming speed, though it doesn't follow you if you move out of its considerable range.

Close combat is out of the question. Your best defense is to avoid them entirely. You can set a Demon on them, but must get close enough to the Mushrooms to wake them up before the Demon can do any damage—they're invulnerable when at rest.

Snark

The waters of Wonderland are populated by these aggressive, legged fish. With their slicing teeth and prehensile tongue, they're the bane of all swimmers. Underwater, Snarks relentlessly chomp on any flesh they can find. If you're on the shore, you may find yourself sucked into the water thanks to a vicious tongue-lashing—there's nothing more alarming than having a fish tongue wrap around your waist and pull you into a dark pond. Finally, be prepared to get a face full of green Snark spit.

The safest course against Snarks is to avoid them entirely or snipe at them from the relative safety of the shore. In the water, use the Vorpal Blade—Snarks usually can't withstand more than one slash of the Blade.

Ladybug

Ladybugs have only one method of attack, but it's a real pain. When you hear their incessant buzzing overhead, be prepared for an exploding acorn to drop on your head. Always look up when you hear them coming and spend quiet moments picking them out of the sky. Not only do the explosions hurt, but the impact can knock you off high ledges.

You'll waste a lot of Strength of Will trying to pin down Ladybugs. Cards often miss and croquet balls are pointless. The most effective weapon is the Vorpal Blade. Though it's difficult to time the knife throws, you'll quickly get the hang of leading these flying targets. They're easiest to hit when they're flying directly at you.

Ant Lion

The Ant Lion is fearsome with its pincers, spiked tail, and mouth filled with long, sharp teeth. Frequently (and especially when attacked), it burrows into the ground. It waits underground until a moment to strike arrives, then leaps out of the earth and latches onto its victim's throat.

Bob and weave when engaging in close combat. After the Ant Lion ducks underground, turn constantly to see the first signs of its resurfacing. The best moments to attack the Ant Lion are when it's burrowing or surfacing, since it's unable to counterattack.

Phantasmagoria

These floating ghosts are unconventional enemies. They attack with spectral chains that momentarily freeze you when they strike. The Phantasmagoria also deprive you of precious Strength of Will, which leaves you open for a vicious finishing attack.

Never stand still when fighting a Phantasmagoria. Their freeze attack is incredibly deadly, especially when there are other enemies in the fray who'll take advantage of your immobilized state.

Fire Imps

Fire Imps are only really dangerous when they attack in groups. Their only attack, a pitchfork stab, is painful but easy to avoid.

A Mallet swing to their little horned skulls or freezing them with the Ice Wand quickly destroys Fire Imps. Just don't let them gang up on you.

Magma Man

Rising from lava pools, these beasts have two equally dangerous states of being. When they emerge from the lava and are still molten, they glow orange and can punch amazing distances. Their touch and the balls of fire they spit can set you ablaze. After they've been on land for a while, Magma Men begin to harden. What they lose in range, they gain in power—the two-fisted pound and uppercut are crushing.

Magma Men are very slow; they're most vulnerable when they're winding up to punch or pound, or when they've just missed with an attack. Take these opportunities to dive in for a quick strike. You can also easily outrun them.

Red Pawns

The Red King's footsoldiers look pretty silly bouncing about on their single foot. You won't be laughing, however, when they head-butt you into the middle of last week. Fortunately, given their lack of arms, this is their only attack.

Attacking from outside head-butt range or directly after a missed strike are safe tactics.

Red Knight

Please don't pet the horses. These sword- and shield-wielding warriors boast a strong but limited attack arsenal.

In the Knight's left hand is a short but sharp sword that he can swing to devastating effect. The other hand holds a shield, which effectively blocks attacks from the right.

Focus on the Knight's left flank or fight from a distance.

Red Bishop

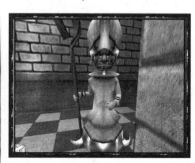

The Red Bishops are relentless and well-armed foes.

Their lengthy staves make dangerous melee weapons when you're anywhere in their reach.

From long distance, Bishops are even more dangerous. Their energy beam attacks are so fast and accurate, they're almost impossible to avoid.

Fight Red Bishops with the Ice Wand, ducking in and out of staff range.

Red Rook

The Rooks' main asset is their bulk, and they know how to use it.

Hand-to-hand combat for Rooks is a bone-crushing jab punch; it's fast and powerful.

Red Rooks don't have a proper projectile attack, but if you retreat out of punch range, they'll rush furiously in your direction with both fists extended.

Pick Red Rooks off from as far away as possible. If they engage you, however, try to stay to their side or behind them to avoid the wrath of their fists.

Clockwork Automaton

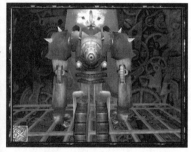

The Mad Hatter's cybernetic creations are a wonder of Victorian engineering.

Their wildly swinging spiked arms deal deep and repeated damage whether you're standing in front or behind. Stay out of arm's reach to avoid this assault.

Harder to avoid is the mid-range steam cloud attack. The burning steam blasts out quickly but can't track you if you avoid it.

From very long distance, the Automatons launch their fists as fast-moving, highly explosive grenades.

The Jacks and Ice Wand are very effective counters to the Automatons' arsenal.

Nightmare Spider

These arachnids are nightmarish indeed. They're also vicious and relentless.

In close combat they slash with their syringe-tipped front legs. Their bite injects venom, which temporarily inflicts partial blindness and disorientation.

Keeping your distance isn't too safe either. The same venom can be spit over long distances, causing severe burns the skin. The Spiders also can cover long distances and get within bite range by spraying webs on the ceiling and swinging right to you.

The Ice Wand is your weapon of choice. It immobilizes the Spider until you stop spraying ice.

Jabberspawn

These smaller, lizard-like children of the Jabberwock can't fly but they can rip you to shreds in a matter of seconds.

Their mighty claws and jaws hack and slash from close range. The beasts can pounce from long distances, using their ragged, sharp talons to slash you to pieces.

You are never safe around a Jabberspawn thanks to its long, whipping tail. Even standing behind it is a dangerous proposition.

The Jabberspawn's projectile attack is a fast-moving lightning attack that can only be avoided with quick reflexes.

Jacks are your weapon of choice, though problems arise when dealing with more than one Jabberspawn. After tossing the Jacks, switch to the Ice Wand to halt any beast that escapes the Jacks.

Spade Card Guard

The Queen's third guard corps is much more deadly than the Diamond and Club Card Guards.

The Spade Card Guards' spears attacks are extremely deadly. The same basic dive-and-weave strategy works with these guards, but you must dodge their attacks quickly.

Their long-distance attack is quite troublesome. They launch spearheads, which detonate in a ball of blue flame. This attack inflicts severe damage and engenders a shock wave that'll knock you back several feet.

Heart Card Guard

The Queen's personal guards are the cream of the crop.

Not only do the Heart Card Guards have hand-to-hand combat attacks that put even the Spade Card Guards to shame, but they possess multiple projectile attacks. Their heart spears can produce dangerous projectiles, which can be used in long distance or close range combat. Plus, they can charge their spears (much like your Eyestaff) for a very fast-moving projectile that detonates in a jarring blast. Attack as they're charging the shot (it takes several seconds) or run toward the projectile as it approaches, sidestepping out of the way at the last moment.

Fire Snark

The lava-dwelling versions of the killer fish are extremely dangerous. Rather than simply spitting nasty green goo, they launch fireballs.

While the Fire Snarks are otherwise the same as their water-dwelling cousins their environment is deadly. Whereas a water Snark could use its tongue to drag you into harmless water, a Fire Snark uses the same appendage to pull you into lava pools. Since there's no way to either anticipate or escape this attack, stay away from lava pools when you see the telltale ripples and smoke indicating the presence of a Fire Snark below the surface.

Enemies—Bosses

Bosses are unique enemies fought in one-on-one battles in large arenas. These fights are usually the culmination of a section of the game. The descriptions below offer general comments on each enemy, including where you can anticipate meeting them. For more detail and tips for victory, see the designated walkthrough chapter.

The Duchess

The Duchess dwells in her makeshift hideout in the Vale of Tears. She'll eat absolutely anything and has no qualms about seasoning, cooking, and eating young girls. You'll need to retrieve the Mock Turtle Shell from the horrible woman's lair by defeating her in combat in "Just Desserts." See "Chapter 6: Vale of Tears."

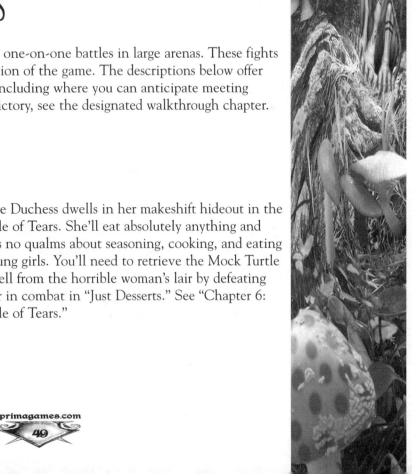

Centipede

This monstrous insect is the leader of the Queen's bug forces. You'll find the Mushroom that allows Alice to regain her normal size in his hellish headquarters. The duel to the death takes place in "Centipede's Sanctum." See "Chapter 7: Wonderland Woods."

Red King

The Red King is the quiet but despotic ruler of the Red Realm. The Queen of Hearts has ordered him to lead the extermination of the inhabitants of the Pale Realm. You'll find that he can move more than one square at a time in your encounter with him in "Checkmate in Red." See "Chapter 8: Looking Glass Land."

Tweedledee and Tweedledum

These corpulent and dim twins have been inexplicably given high rank in the Mad Hatter's operation. They run the twisted madhouse in "Mirror Image." See "Chapter 8: Looking Glass Land."

Mad Hatter

Having gone totally insane, the Mad Hatter now dedicates himself to not only tea but to creating mechanically perfect cybernetic soldiers. His abominations are on display in his horrific funhouse just before your battle with him in "About Face." See "Chapter 9: Behind the Looking Glass."

Jabberwock

The ferocious Jabberwock is the Queen's gatekeeper. This winged horror knows what you fear and uses it to his benefit in two different encounters. Battle him first in "Jabberwock's Lair" and again in "Royal Rage." When you finally vanquish the Jabberwock, you'll hear faint cheers of "Callooh, Callay!" See "Chapters 10: Land of Fire and Brimstone" and "Chapter 12: Queensland."

Queen of Hearts 1

In the first of two climactic encounters with the Queen of Hearts, she appears as a nightmarish version of herself. Rooted to her throne by a gigantic tentacle, she has become infused with the most fear-inspiring powers you'll face in all of Wonderland. This most difficult of all battles occurs in "Heart of Darkness." See "Chapter 12: Queensland."

Queen of Hearts 2

Not a woman who takes defeat lightly, the Queen refuses to die, fighting you instead in a netherworld arena in her true form. Floating in the center as a towering, blood-spewing tentacled titan, the Queen is the perfect final opponent. Beat her and Alice regains her Sanity. The final battle takes place in "Heart of Darkness." See "Chapter 12: Queensland."

Friends

These characters offer varying levels of assistance and guidance in the trials and adventures that lay ahead. A girl can always use a good friend when facing personal demons and ultimate evil.

Cheshire Cat

The Cheshire Cat is your constant companion. Not only does he provide unsolicited guidance throughout your adventure, but he also provides advice on request. It's not always easy to understand, but it's comforting nevertheless.

Miner

These short and understandably downtrodden laborers inhabit the mines of the Village of the Doomed. One of them provides you with your first mission: finding the Mayor.

Mayor Elder

The Mayor, while hiding in the mines in "Pandemonium," tells you where to find the shrinking potion you'll need. He'll be your guide through the Fortress of Doors.

Mock Turtle

The Mock Turtle agrees to an exchange that results in Alice gaining the ability to dive underwater. He'll be your guide through much of the Vale of Tears and will escort you to the Wonderland Woods.

Bill McGill (a.k.a. Larry)

This chameleon hasn't come very far from his chimney-diving days. His home has been sullied by the Duchess's headquarters and he'll gladly help you find and destroy her.

White Rabbit

The White Rabbit is a bit twitchy and rushed, but he's a good friend. He summons you to return and liberate Wonderland but, in typical fashion, gets too far ahead of you. Finding him again is an adventure in itself.

Caterpillar

The Caterpillar is back and is as vague as ever. With Rabbit's guidance, you must locate Caterpillar to understand the nature of your mission. He also reappears in a mysterious but not unexpected form.

White King

The White King is under siege and is grateful for your help. He needs you to rescue the captured White Queen from the village of the Red King.

The Dormouse and the March Hare

These two loonies have become the hapless victims of the even more deeply insane Hatter. Strapped to surgical tables in the Hatter's nightmarish funhouse, they don't even seem to realize they've been turned nearly inside out. There's a grain of truth in what they say, but most of it is nonsense.

Gryphon

This dignified and courageous captive of the Hatter is a valuable ally. Free him from the funhouse, and he'll lead the forces of good Wonderland against the Queen. He is invaluable in your battles against the Jabberwock.

Non-Combatants

Non-combatants wander Wonderland, but mean you no harm. Attacking them is pointless, as you cannot harm them.

Walking Rocks

Don't waste your valuable time and Strength of Will fighting these invulnerable inhabitants of the deep underbrush. Their only danger to you is that they might distract your summoned Demons from attacking their proper targets.

Insane Children

The most unfortunate victims of the Queen's reign of terror are the Insane Children that wander all over Wonderland. There's nothing you can do for (or to) them.

part II
Walkthroughs

Chapter 4
Village of the Doomed

T he Village of the Doomed is your first indication that something is very wrong in Wonderland. The people are sullen, the air is thick with evil, and living, pulsating tentacles penetrate the earth.

Your brief stay here serves as basic training for the more intense challenges to come. Take your time and learn the ropes now when the pressure is light.

In this region of Wonderland you'll meet:

Friends:	**Foes:**
♣ White Rabbit	♣ Club Card Guards
♣ Cheshire Cat	♣ Diamond Card Guards
♣ Miners	
♣ Mayor Elder	

To boost your budding arsenal of deadly Toys, you'll find:

♣ Vorpal Blade

♣ Cards

Dementia

Bottom of the Hole

Safely at the bottom of the rabbit hole, you reunite with the White Rabbit and the Cheshire Cat. Walk forward into the mineshaft. Follow the shaft, turning right and walk down a short flight of stairs.

Follow the shaft.

Wrong Side of the Bridge

The mineshaft opens into a large room; diminutive Miners are hard at work. Talk to the small fellow working nearby.

Drat! That bridge was the easy way across.

As you complete this conversation, a large fleshy tentacle takes out the bridge that traverses the toxic stream below. You have to find another way across.

Line up with the remaining planks of the destroyed bridge, back up, and take a running leap across the toxic stream. The steam rising from the stream gives you the extra lift you need to reach the other side where you find Drole Vel's Gas Extraction.

Jump from the broken planks of the bridge and use the steam jet to float to the opposite side.

Note

THIS WON'T BE THE LAST TIME YOU USE STEAM VENTS TO GET ACROSS WIDE GAPS. REMEMBER THE EXPERIENCE.

Drole Vel's Gas Extraction

At Drole Vel's Gas Extraction, chat with the Miner, then walk down the only available passage.

Go down the next passage near the Gas Extraction shop.

At the first turn, the Cheshire Cat shows you a bit of Meta-Essence. Pick it up—that fall into Dementia hurt!

The Cheshire Cat points out your first bit of Meta-Essence.

Turn right. Pick up the Vorpal Blade at the top of the ramp.

The Vorpal Blade is your basic Toy.

New Toy: Vorpal Blade

VORPAL BLADE

THE VORPAL BLADE IS YOUR BASIC WEAPON. THOUGH IT IS A TOY, IT'S NOT RECOMMENDED FOR CHILDREN UNDER THE AGE OF THREE DUE TO ITS RAZOR SHARP BLADE.

USE IT PRIMARILY TO HACK AND SLASH. YOU CAN THROW IT, BUT YOU'RE DEPRIVED OF ITS USE FOR SEVERAL SECONDS AFTER THE TOSS.

Mayor Elder's House and Rana Mushroom Shop

Stroll down the ramp. As you reach the first platform, Rabbit shrinks and hops through a very small door in the wall. Looks like you can't follow him any farther. Not that way, at least.

Just as Rabbit disappears, a Club Card Guard arrives. Climb the ramp and "cut the deck."

Rabbit inconsiderately goes where you cannot.

A Club Card Guard is your first foe.

New Foe: Club Card Guard

CLUB CARD GUARD

ATTACK CLUB CARD GUARDS BY SIDE-STEPPING BACK AND FORTH. DODGE OR JUMP TO AVOID THEIR SPEAR STABS AND IMMEDIATELY COUNTER-ATTACK.

GET BEHIND THE CLUB CARD GUARDS; THEY CAN'T ATTACK FROM THE REAR AND THEY'RE SLOW TO TURN BECAUSE OF THEIR CRIPPLING TWO-DIMENSIONALITY.

Chat with the Miner in front of Mayor Elder's house.

Turn right at the Rana Mushroom Shop and go through the door to the Buzzed Sawmill.

Tip

IF YOU DIN'T PICK IT UP BEFORE, GO BACK FOR THAT FIRST META-ESSENCE.

Go right at the Rana Mushroom Shop.

The Buzzed Sawmill

Creep straight ahead. Turn left and jump to grab the high ledge. If you're not sure where to jump, look for the Cat. Once Alice has a good hold, press Forward to pull her the rest of the way up.

Jump up to grab the ledge where the Cat appears.

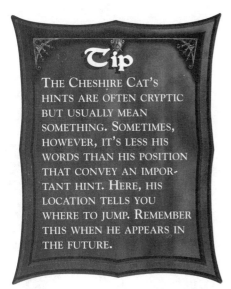

Tip

THE CHESHIRE CAT'S HINTS ARE OFTEN CRYPTIC BUT USUALLY MEAN SOMETHING. SOMETIMES, HOWEVER, IT'S LESS HIS WORDS THAN HIS POSITION THAT CONVEY AN IMPORTANT HINT. HERE, HIS LOCATION TELLS YOU WHERE TO JUMP. REMEMBER THIS WHEN HE APPEARS IN THE FUTURE.

Traverse the ledge and go up the first ramp to talk to the Miner. The shrinking secret you seek is in the Fortress of Doors. Look deeper in the Mine to find someone who helps you get inside.

Turn left and climb a short ramp to another landing.

Climb the first two ramps, stopping to talk to the Miner.

Look right and jump down to the platform leading to "Yur Mine." Again, the location of the Cat serves as your clue for where to go next.

Go through the doorway to move to the next level.

Jump down to the Cat to move on to the next level.

Pandemonium

Meeting Mayor Elder

Step froward and drop onto a high platform.

Turn right and jump to the nearest rope.

Jump to the rope to make your way to the ground below.

Get the rope swinging toward the platform below. Once you have a good, long swing, jump.

The rope allows you to take a nice, long leap.

> ### Tip
>
> TO GET THE ROPE SWINGING, PRESS AND HOLD FORWARD. WHEN ALICE STARTS MOVING BACKWARD, RELEASE IT AND WAIT UNTIL SHE STARTS MOVING FORWARD. THEN, PRESS FORWARD AGAIN TO GAIN MOMENTUM.
>
> REPEAT THIS PROCESS UNTIL SHE IS SWINGING SUFFICIENTLY TO MAKE THE JUMP.

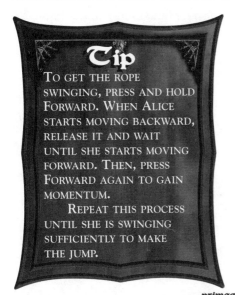

Prima's Official Strategy Guide

> **Note**
>
> AFTER YOU LAND, YOU NOTICE THE AREA TO YOUR LEFT (AND A WARP PORTAL IN THE DISTANCE). YOU'RE FREE TO CHECK IT OUT, BUT THERE'S NO POINT, YET. YOU'LL FIND YOUR WAY THERE SOON ENOUGH.

Turn right and stroll down the ramp to meet with Mayor Elder. He asks you to retrieve a key from the Card Guards' Compound. In exchange, he helps you find a way to become small in the Fortress of Doors.

The Mayor is the man you seek.

The Ramp to the Elevator

Go through the doorway behind the Mayor into the heart of "Yur Mine" (note the sign).

Turn left and climb up the ramp. You need to sidestep very cautiously to move between parts of the ramp. You don't want to fall!

Heed the sign ("Danger") and climb carefully up the ramps.

At the top of the ramp, step on the elevator. Sit back and watch Alice's wild ride on the runaway mine cart. Don't worry, she has enough sense to know when to disembark.

Whee! Sit back and watch the ride.

Alice hops off when the tracks run out.

Outside the Card Guard Compound

Turn around and slaughter the Club Card Guard waiting up the ramp.

Cards are useful Toys for long-distance combat.

Look for the Cards floating to the left of the wooden door.

New Toy: Cards

CARD

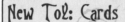

QUICKLY TOSS CARDS ONE AT A TIME AT A DISTANT TARGET OR FIRE SEVERAL FOR A MORE SHOTGUN-LIKE EFFECT.

Pick up the Cards and head through the doorway to the Card Guards' Compound.

Card Guards' Compound

The Compound is lousy with Card Guards, including the long-range attacking Diamond Card Guard.

Wind around the stairs and try out your new Toy on the Diamond Card Guard and two Club Card Guards.

New Foe: Diamond Card Guard

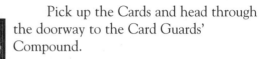

DIAMOND CARD GUARD

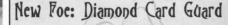

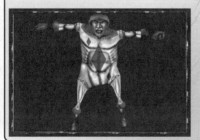

DIAMOND CARD GUARDS CAN FIRE RIGHT BACK AT YOU. DUCK BEHIND STRUCTURES TO AVOID DAMAGE. THESE PROJECTILES DON'T TRACK PARTICULARLY WELL, HOWEVER. IN CLOSE RANGE, BEWARE THE GUARDS' BUZZ SAW STAFFS AND QUICK SPINNING MOVE.

Grab the key off the table and a door opens nearby.

Climb the stairs and go through the doorway to enter your first transport portal.

Jump onto the table to grab the key the Mayor desires.

The doorway leads to a transport portal.

Meeting the Mayor, Again

Peek out the doorway and snipe at the two Diamond Card Guards on the high platforms.

Eviscerate the Card Guards before trying to cross this room.

Jump on the front porch and onto the rope.

You may need to shimmy up the rope a bit (press Use) before leaping to the dock.

Walk down the ramp to meet with the Mayor. Since you've fulfilled your part of the bargain, he takes you to the Fortress of Doors.

Use the rope to get to the dock.

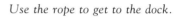

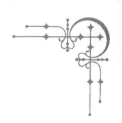

Chapter 5
Fortress of Doors

The Fortress of Doors tests your ability to adjust to the unfamiliar terrain of Wonderland. After a pretty conventional beginning, things start to get a little hazy, and you quickly realize that you aren't dealing with a world that behaves as you expect. The Fortress and the Skool within are massive structural puzzles that defy spatial logic and any conventional sense of direction. Have fun, and don't get lost.

FORTRESS OF DOORS

In this region of Wonderland you'll find:

Friends:
- ♣ Mayor Elder

Foes:
- ♣ Club Card Guards
- ♣ Diamond Card Guards
- ♣ Boojums

To boost your budding arsenal of deadly Toys, you'll find:

- ♣ Cards
- ♣ Croquet Mallet

Fortress of Doors

Outside the Wall

The long ride in the Mayor's blimp ends with Alice leaping to a narrow ledge outside the Fortress of Doors.

Walk straight ahead and duck into the hole in the Fortress wall to the right.

Stroll forward and look for the hole in the wall that gets you inside the Fortress.

Note

IF YOU GO AROUND THE FRONT OF THE FORTRESS, YOU'LL MEET A DIAMOND CARD GUARD AND FIND A SERIES OF PLATFORMS TO JUMP ON. UNFORTUNATELY, THEY DON'T LEAD ANYWHERE. DON'T WASTE YOUR TIME UNLESS YOU WANT SOME JUMPING PRACTICE.

Inside the Walls

Inside the walls, you find the Skool the Mayor referred to. It floats in the middle of the Fortress, inaccessible from this area.

The Skool is an imposing presence in the Fortress. You need to go through several more doors before you can get inside.

> ## Tip
>
> DON'T FRET OVER THE CARD GUARDS ON THE WALL ABOVE YOU. YOU EVENTUALLY FIND YOUR WAY TO THE TOP OF THE WALL LATER IN THIS SECTION.

The only option is through the doorway opposite the Skool. Jump over the fallen blocks and duck inside the doorway.

Look for the only door out of this courtyard, but don't pass through until you're ready. There's no going back.

> ## Note
>
> YOUR RATIONAL MIND MAY TELL YOU THAT THIS DOOR IS THE FRONT GATE TO THE FORTRESS, WHICH LEADS BACK OUTSIDE. TELL YOUR RATIONAL MIND TO TAKE A FLYING LEAP—IT HAS NO ROLE HERE. IN WONDERLAND, THIS DOOR LEADS TO AN ENTIRELY DIFFERENT PLACE.

The Separating Room

Other than the swirling sky, the room *looks* normal enough. It's not!

Turn to face the staircase on the other side of the room and run as fast as you can.

At some point, the floor starts to split open and the halves of the room separate. If it looks like you might lose the floor under Alice's feet, jump the rest of the way.

Note

IF YOU MISSED THE CARDS IN THE PREVIOUS AREA, PICK THEM UP IN THE ALCOVE ON THE SAME SIDE OF THE ROOM AS THE DOOR.

When the room starts to separate, jump.

Know what you're doing before you make this jump. Once you go, you need to move quickly.

Once you're safely on the other side, take a moment to catch your breath, then scale the spiral staircase to the upper level of the room.

There are two ways to handle the next part: You can run and fight, or simply run. Given the double dose of Boojums patrolling the air and the large possibility of plummeting into an infinite abyss, running is the best course of action.

New Foe: Boojum

BOOJUM

THE BOOJUM IS A MENACE IN THE AIR. ITS WEAPON IS A SCREAM THAT INFLICTS DAMAGE AND PUSHES ALICE IN THE DIRECTION OF THE SCREAM. BECAUSE BOOJUMS LURK AROUND PRECARIOUS LEDGES, THE DANGER THEY POSE TO ALICE IS OBVIOUS.

THE BEST WAY TO FIGHT THEM IS FROM A VERY GREAT DISTANCE. OTHERWISE, MOVE CONSTANTLY (ESPECIALLY WHEN IN THE PATH OF THE SCREAM) AND STAY AWAY FROM LEDGES.

After you jump to the walkway, it starts to tip under your weight. Run to avoid the Boojums. Don't stop until you're safely on the ledge on the other side of the room.

The walkway tilts like an S-shaped seesaw.

Warning

DON'T FIGHT THE BOOJUMS WHILE ON THE WALKWAY. ONE SCREAM WILL KNOCK YOU OFF.

If the walkway is higher than the ledge, jump quickly. If not, run back to retilt the walkway and try again.

On the other side, dive into the transport portal.

Tip

IF, YOU ARRIVE AT THE OTHER END OF THE WALK-WAY AND THE END IS TOO LOW TO MAKE THE JUMP, RETURN TO THE BEGINNING AND LET THE WALKWAY TILT AS FAR AS IT WILL GO. THEN, RUN AS FAST AS YOU CAN TO MAKE THE JUMP.

Head into the portal. There are plenty more Boojums later.

Beyond the Wall

The Rage Room

The room ahead is chock full of Card Guards. There is, however, a little treat in the center of the room that makes it much easier.

Arm your Blade and rush into the center of the room. Hop onto the platform and activate the Rage Box. While it's active, you do increased damage and receive very little. Let the slaughter begin.

Look for the platform in the center of the room to find the first Rage Box.

The Rage Box is one powerful power-up.

Off with their heads!

After all the Club Card Guards are decapitated or sliced in half, explore the room.

Head through the door beyond the Rage Box. Continue through three more doors.

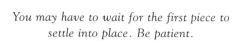

*The exit is on the opposite side
of the Rage Room.*

Dancing Floor Room

Across the vast divide is the other half of
the room. Periodically, pieces of the floor
dance from the other side of the room to
your side. Wait for a piece to fall into
place in front of the ledge and step
onto it.

When you reach the other side then,
get your back against a wall and wait for
the Boojum to attack. Let loose with the
deck of Cards and deal a killer hand.

*You may have to wait for the first piece to
settle into place. Be patient.*

Warning

BEWARE, AS FLOOR PIECES ARE ADDED IN FRONT OF YOU, THEY'RE ALSO FALLING AWAY BEHIND YOU. MAKE SURE YOU'RE NOT STANDING ON A PIECE WHEN IT DECIDES TO DEPART.

This crossing requires considerable patience. If you see the floor beneath your feet begin to give, step onto another square to await the next floor pieces.

Move carefully across the floor and wait for pieces to assemble to make easy jumps.

There are two solid islands in the abyss. Don't pause for too long or you have to wait for the whole process to recycle.

The solid islands offer a place to catch your breath, but only briefly.

Three-Tone Room

As you arrive in the next area, you see a vision of three doors closing on the opposite side of another nightmarish abyss. Listen carefully as they close; you need to remember the sequence of tones.

Immediately turn your attention to vaporizing the pair of Boojums defending this room.

Note the switch here. If you get the door sequence wrong, reset the puzzle with this switch. It also replays the tune you must emulate.

Go down the spiral staircase and pull the three switches in this order:

1. Right
2. Left
3. Middle

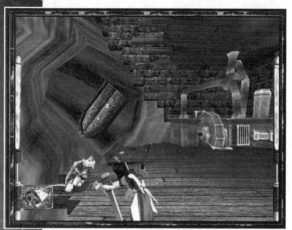

These three switches must be pulled in the correct order.

Return to the upper level and approach the ledge; a piece of checkerboard floor awaits. Unlike in the previous room, the floor tiles here rise as you need them. Step onto the first and the next appears.

Before you go, mow down the Diamond and Club Card Guards on the opposite side of the abyss. You don't want to be knocked off by a Diamond Card Guard's projectile.

Near the other end of the abyss, jump to the platform.

Walk through the doors, and bob and weave with the Diamond Card Guard manning the portal.

Dive into the portal.

A Diamond Card Guard fiercely guards the portal.

The Rising Floor Room

As you enter, this seemingly normal room erupts into chaos. The floor begins to spin and rise and fall. Two Club Card Guards ride the floor tiles, awaiting your arrival.

Jump to the first piece directly in front of you.

Eventually, the piece you're standing on briefly meets up with the piece directly in front of it. Walk across while the pieces are fleetingly connected.

Tip

TAKE THIS OPPORTUNITY TO USE YOUR CARDS AGAINST THE WAITING CARD GUARDS.

Wait for this first tile to meet with the one in front of it and walk across to the new piece.

Tip

VIEWING THE ACTION FROM ABOVE MAKES THIS MUCH EASIER AND REDUCES THE CHANCE OF FALLING.

Repeat this process across the room. There's no one way to get across.

After you reach the last piece before the landing, back up as much as possible to get a running jump. You probably have to pull yourself up by your fingertips.

After you reach solid ground, pass through the portal.

It's a long jump to the ledge, so don't be surprised if you have to hang on.

Three Door Monte

This room is the upper portion of the Rage Room. Three platforms jut out from your current location. At the end of each is a door. Periodically, the three doors switch positions. Before any switching begins, the door on the right conceals an entrance to a portal. Even if it moves, you'll know it by its green color.

Dance with the Boojums. Once the coast is clear, explore the area.

If the doors shift while you're standing nearby, be sure you aren't standing too close when the new one lands; they're heavy and they don't care who they crush.

When the door opens, a portal reveals itself. Dive in quickly.

Note

IF YOU FALL INTO THE RAGE ROOM BELOW, LOOK FOR THE RISING PLATFORM TO GET BACK UP.

*Pick the door that conceals
a portal. Go green.*

Fortress of Doors (Return)

Sneak out of the parapet and unload on the two Diamond Card Guards.

*You find yourself on the wall around the
Fortress. Don't go past this point until you've
vanquished both Card Guards.*

Warning

DO NOT GO BEYOND THE FIRST CORNER OF THE WALKWAY BEFORE YOU'VE ELIMINATED THE CARD GUARDS. DEALING WITH THE CARD GUARDS *PLUS* A PAIR OF BOOJUMS IS TOO DIFFICULT.

After you round the first corner, two Boojums fly out of an open window on the far side of the Skool.

The Boojums serve as a big hint about where you should go next. That open window is the only way into the Skool.

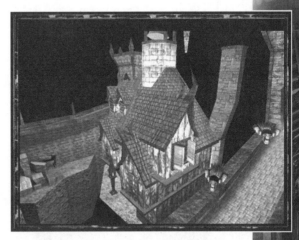

Note

IF YOU FALL OFF THE WALL, CLIMB THE PILE OF FALLEN BLOCKS TO GET BACK UP.

Shoot down both Boojums and head around the wall to the open window.

Jump onto the lip of the wall and wait for the Skool to drift down to its lowest point. After it begins drifting back up, jump to the sill to return to the rigors of lower education.

Note

IF YOU DIDN'T PICK THEM UP BEFORE, CARDS CAN BE FOUND IN THE PARAPET ON THE FAR END OF THE WALL.

Start your jump to the Skool by hopping onto the lip of the wall. The Jump indicator comes in handy here.

Skool Daze

Main Foyer

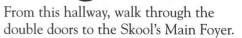

From this hallway, walk through the double doors to the Skool's Main Foyer.

Pause to take care of a little business with a squad of Card Guards.

Stay in the hall and use the doorway as cover to fight the several Diamond and Club Card Guards who flood to greet you.

The Foyer has two floors.

The first floor features a large, imposing fireplace. Left of it is the door to the Theater.

Behind the staircase and down a ramp is a locked double door.

Warning

BEWARE THE HOLE IN THE FLOOR.

Upstairs, all but two doors are boarded up. One swings slightly open and closed but is inaccessible. The other, nearest the staircase, leads to the Library.

First, turn left and approach the fireplace. Jump toward it to grab hold of the low portion of the mantle. Pull up and turn left.

Jump up to hang on the fireplace mantel and pull yourself up.

Jump to the isolated ledge to pick up the Croquet Mallet.

A new Toy awaits.

New Toy: Croquet Mallet

CROQUET MALLET

THE CROQUET MALLET IS A GREAT WEAPON. THE PRIMARY ATTACK IS A CLUB SWING WITH AN ELECTRIC CHARGE KICKER. IT'S A POTENT HIT BUT IT TAKES A WHILE TO STRIKE. AGAINST VERY QUICK OPPONENTS, YOU TAKE A LOT OF DAMAGE GETTING IN JUST A FEW SWINGS. START YOUR WIND-UP AS YOU RUSH TOWARD A FOE AND THE SWING WILL ARRIVE JUST AS YOU COME INTO ATTACK RANGE.

IN ALTERNATE ATTACK MODE, THE MALLET REALLY SHINES. ALICE TOSSES A CROQUET BALL INTO THE AIR AND SMACKS IT, GOLF-STYLE, TOWARD THE TARGET INDICATOR. IF IT HITS A WALL, THE BALL BOUNCES AROUND THE ROOM UNTIL IT HITS ALICE OR AN ENEMY. AGAIN, THIS ATTACK TAKES A LONG TIME TO LAUNCH, BUT YOU CAN MOVE WHILE ALICE WINDS UP.

Jump back to the ground and go into the Theater (door left of the fireplace).

Take the door to the Theater.

Theater

Briefly chat with the Mayor. He directs you to find the Book of Bizarre Things. Suddenly two Diamond Card Guards rush in to break up the meeting.

This charming Skool play is broken up by the arrival of Card Guards.

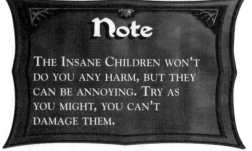

Note

THE INSANE CHILDREN WON'T DO YOU ANY HARM, BUT THEY CAN BE ANNOYING. TRY AS YOU MIGHT, YOU CAN'T DAMAGE THEM.

Return to the Main Foyer.

Main Foyer

Trudge upstairs and enter the door to the Library.

Library, Entry Hall

Use your new Mallet on the two Club Card Guards and pass through the second set of double doors.

Go left at the T-intersection.

A Diamond Card Guard rushes in from the end of the hall. A Club Card Guard lurks in an alcove to the left.

At the end of the hall, turn right and enter the Library's First Floor.

The door to the Library is fiercely guarded.

Library, First Floor

Your goal is to find four flying books that form a path to the Book of Bizarre Things.

Begin searching the first floor on the left side. One Club Card Guard shouldn't be any trouble.

Look in the distance for a blue light glowing in the stacks. When you approach, the book springs to life and flies to the top of the room. That's one.

The first flying book. As with all four, it glows bright blue in the half-light of the Library.

Jump onto the spiral elevator near where you entered the room and ride it to the second floor.

The spiral elevator is the only way to the second floor.

Library, Second Floor

Begin by examining the left side.

The Cat provides an avenue to the third floor by tipping over a bookshelf on the right side. Don't go up to the third floor, yet.

STEPS TO ENLIGHTENMENT BRIGHTEN THE WAY; BUT THE STEPS ARE STEEP. TAKE THEM ONE AT A TIME.

The Cat opens the way to the next floor.

You find the second book to the left. Approach it to set it in motion.

The second book is just to the left of the elevator.

You have to battle a Diamond Card Guard and two Club Card Guards on this side of the room.

Tip

WHILE YOU'RE HERE, THE CAT TOPPLES TWO BOOK-SHELVES. THIS GIVES YOU ACCESS TO THE OBSERVATORY, WHICH IS ON THE THIRD FLOOR, RIGHT SIDE, BEHIND A LOCKED, STAR-EMBLAZONED DOOR.

Dig around in the stacks on the right side of the room and clear out a Club Card Guard before proceeding up the toppled bookshelf to the third floor.

Jump onto the fallen bookcase and climb to the next floor.

Library, Third Floor

At the top of the bookshelf, dance with some Diamond Card Guards and activate the flying book nearby.

From the book, proceed forward to find an elevator to the fourth floor.

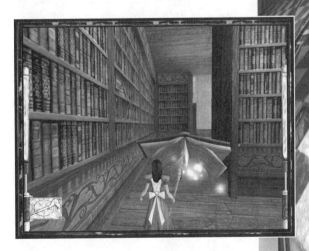

The third book. Keep walking forward to find the elevator to the next floor.

This elevator takes you to the fourth and final floor.

Library, Fourth Floor

Turn around as you ride up and be ready to fight a Diamond Card Guard.

Don't be caught napping as you arrive at the fourth floor.

Step off the elevator to activate the final flying book.

Continue straight ahead from the elevator and notice the path made by the flying books.

Step onto the first one.

Jump onto each of the three remaining books until you reach the shelf with the Book of Bizarre Things.

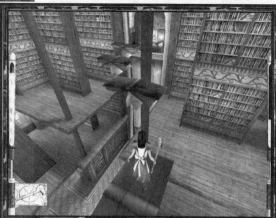

This path of books leads to the tome you seek.

Leap to the shelf containing the gigantic Book of Bizarre Things.

Alice and the Cat find a way to open the locked book. Go back down there and read it.

The flying books reconfigure to allow Alice to jump down to either side of the third floor. Go left.

Take the book path leading left and get down to floor level to read the book.

Work your way back down to the floor and read the Book of Bizarre Things.

Mushrooms, Poppies, Sugar, and Spice are the ingredients you seek for the shrinking potion. Time to go find them.

The shrinking potion recipe seems easy.

MUSHROOMS, POPPIES, SUGAR AND SPICE ALL THOSE THINGS ARE VERY NICE. WHEN COMBINED THE PROPER MIXTURE MAKES A GETTING SMALL

Skool's Out

Spiral Atrium

You find yourself in a large, three-story atrium. The third floor is apparently inaccessible.

Emerge from the alcove to meet immediately with a very perturbed Boojum.

The first floor features doors on either side. On the left is a door illuminated with a white light. Go there first.

Start with the door with white lights.

Dice Room

Carefully descend the stairs to a landing overlooking another abyss. Across the abyss is a small, isolated chunk of room with a new Toy glowing on it. Guarding this coveted item is a Boojum.

Hit the Boojum before he notices you.

Next, approach the abyss carefully and look down to the right. Another Boojum waits in the darkness below (you only see him if your Target indicator acquires him).

Don't claim the Toy until both Boojums are immolated.

Jump across using the longest of the ragged floorboards.

The Demon Dice and one of two lurking Boojums wait on the distant platform.

After you reach the platform, grab the Demon Dice and return to the Spiral Atrium.

The Demon Dice will look nice in the Toy chest.

New Toy: Demon Dice

DEMON DICE

THE DEMON DICE HAVE TREMENDOUS POWER BUT YOU MUST USE THEM WISELY. IN PRIMARY ATTACK MODE, USE THEIR TARGETING SYSTEM EXACTLY AS YOU WOULD THE JUMP INDICATOR. WHEN YOU'RE READY TO TOSS THEM, PRESS THE PRIMARY ATTACK BUTTON. A DEMON WILL BE SUMMONED TO AUTOMATICALLY ATTACK NEARBY ENEMIES. HE PERSISTS UNTIL DEFEATED OR UNTIL HE'S NO LONGER NEEDED.

DON'T USE THE DICE WHEN THERE ARE NO ENEMIES ABOUT. DEMONS ATTACK THE FIRST TARGET THEY SEE WHICH, IN SUCH A CASE, IS ALICE.

DEMON DICE ARE UNIQUE AMONG THE TOYS: COLLECTING SEVERAL OF THEM GIVES THE TOY GREATER POWER. LATER, WHEN YOU HAVE COLLECTED TWO OR THREE DICE, YOU CAN SUMMON INCREASINGLY POWERFUL DEMONS. FOR NOW YOU HAVE TO BE CONTENT WITH THE LESSER DEMON AND HIS LIGHTNING BOLT ATTACK.

Spiral Atrium

Cross to the other side of the first floor and pass through the doors marked by the red lights.

Surprise the Diamond Card Guard manning this T-intersection and go through either door to the Gymnasium.

The door with red lights is your next stop.

Gymnasium

Climb the ramp to the stage and investigate the room to the left.

Next, enter the room on the right. Pull the switch to extend the retractable bleachers in the main area of the gym.

Climb the bleachers and turn around to jump to the beams crisscrossing the ceiling. Jump from the first beam to the broken beam extending from the center of the room.

Hop up to this jagged beam.

Pause at the first junction of the beams and wait for the swinging lamp to pass before crossing.

Wait for the lamp to pass before continuing.

Tip

DON'T GRAB THE RAGE BOX YET.

Keep your eyes peeled for the Mayor.

Continue over the beams until you reach the Mayor waiting in the far corner of the room. He has the shrinking potion's first ingredient: the Mushroom.

You're interrupted by the arrival of several Boojums ambling up through the hole in the floor.

Rush back to the Rage Box and use it before leaping down to the relative safety of the gym floor.

Use your enhanced powers to do away with the Boojums, then return to the Spiral Atrium.

The Rage Box makes the Boojum trio a bit more manageable.

Spiral Atrium

Climb to the second floor.

Sweep the area for Card Guards before entering the door marked "2nd Grayd."

As soon as the door opens, fling in the Demon Dice to deal with the Card Guards.

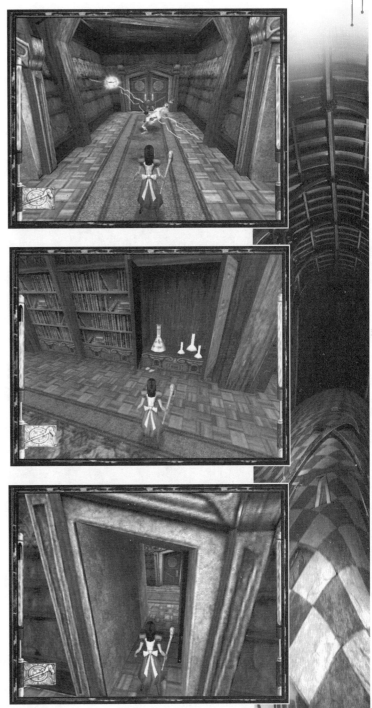

The hall to the 2nd Grayd Classroom is a great time to test the Demon Dice.

2nd Grayd Classroom

Enter the doors at the end of the hall. Two Club Card Guards are attacking the helpless Mayor.

The ungrateful little man tells you he's got the Sugared Spice Drops called for in the recipe. Now, all you need are the Poppies.

Grab the bottle of Jumbo Grow out of the nearby cabinet.

Take the Jumbo Grow out of the cabinet before you leave.

Return to the hall and go through either of the side doors. They both lead to the third floor. This is Wonderland … do try to keep that in mind.

Both of the second floor side hall doors lead to the third floor hallway.

3rd Grayd Classroom

Clobber the Diamond Card Guard and two Club Card Guards. Enter the doors leading to the 3rd Grayd Classroom.

Two Diamond Card Guards are protecting the door to the Greenhouse and, on the far side of the classroom, a Croquet Mallet (if you didn't grab it before).

This door marks the way you want to go.

Greenhouse

Storm through the double doors to the Greenhouse. Kill the Boojum and two Club Card Guards.

Walk straight into the room and look for the bed labeled "Poppy Seeds." Pour the Jumbo Grow on the seeds and your prize suddenly springs from the earth. Jump to the bed to pick the odd flower.

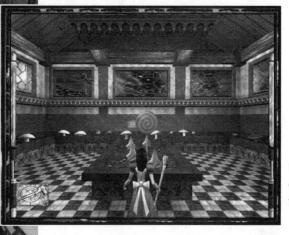

Pour the Jumbo Grow on the seeds to get the final potion ingredient.

Leave the Greenhouse and return to the third floor hallway. Go through either of the side doors to return to the second floor hallway.

2nd Grald Classroom

Meet again with the Mayor and he whips up your shrinking potion. Don't leave without picking up the potion (labeled "Drink Me") and the Observatory key (the star).

Whatever you do, don't forget the shrinking potion and the star.

Walk into the portal to return to the Main Atrium.

Skool Daze, Return

Main Atrium

Starting at the locked door below the stairs, fight through the newly arrived Diamond and Club Card Guards and get to the second floor of the Library.

You find reinforcements have arrived in the Main Atrium and the Library.

Library, Second Floor

Head to the left side of the floor.
Hop onto the toppled bookshelf and scale it to the third floor.

Hop onto the toppled bookcase on the left side of the second floor and climb up to the third floor.

Gut the Diamond and Club Card

Tip

THERE ARE DIAMOND CARD GUARDS SNIPING AT YOU FROM ALL ANGLES, SO WORK FAST AND KEEP MOVING. DON'T STOP TO FIGHT.

Guards patrolling near the Observatory and enter the star-emblazoned door.

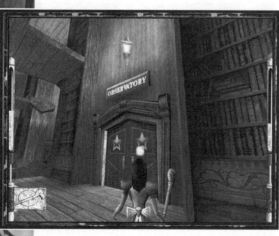

The Observatory door.

Observatory

Ride the elevator and stroll through the next set of double doors.

Deal out the Club and Diamond Club Card Guards on the first floor and scale the steps to the second. The Diamond Card Guard on the top floor will likely jump down for a piece of the action. Give him all the trouble he can handle.

Clear out all of the stargazing Card Guards before heading upstairs.

Scale the steps to the second floor, jumping over the broken stairs.

Climb the ramp to the eyepiece of the telescope.

Watch out for the broken stairs.

Climb up to the telescope to reveal the exit.

The globe in the center of the room opens to reveal a portal. Alice drinks her shrinking potion and dives into the portal.

Chapter 6
The Vale of Tears

In this region of Wonderland you'll meet:

Friends:

♣ Mock Turtle

♣ Bill McGill

♣ Caterpillar

Foes:

♣ Ladybug

♣ Army Ant Solider

♣ Blood Rose

♣ Snark

♣ Army Ant Commander

♣ Evil Mushroom

♣ Duchess (boss)

To boost your budding arsenal of deadly Toys, you'll find:

♣ Jackbomb

Pool of Tears

The Waterfall

Life as a very small person begins at the base of a gigantic waterfall. Of course, it's probably just a trickle from a rivulet, but why quibble with scale? At your current size, blades of grass loom above your head and mere insects are towering enemies.

Begin by trudging down to the left side of the fall.

Note the "Beware of Falling Rocks" sign and jump over the chasm to the pathway.

Climb past the waterfall to the far end of the cliff.

Falling rocks indeed. The sign doesn't lie.

At the first switchback, pull up to continue.

Scale the ledge, turn around, and jump the gap to continue on the path up the falls.

Jump over the ledge in front of the falls and pause there.

> # Note
>
> THE WALKING ROCKS MEAN YOU NO HARM, BUT THEY'RE ALSO INDESTRUCTIBLE. DON'T WASTE YOUR STRENGTH OF WILL ON THEM.

Wait for the rock to fall before going any farther.

An Army Ant Soldier pushes a rock down the falls. Wait here and it falls harmlessly in front of you.

Take the next jump and climb up the ledge to reach the next switchback.

Turn around and jump up to the path.

After you reach the falls, the Army Ants send another rock your way. Rush back to the switchback and wait for the rock to fall down the gap in front of you.

Return to the last switchback after you see the next rock coming.

Resume your trek, jumping past the waterfall a third time.

Continue until you reach the next switchback. Look up to see two Ladybugs fluttering in the air above. Open fire as quickly as possible; those acorns they're carrying explode on impact.

New Foe: Ladybug

LADYBUG

THESE FLYING INSECTS ARE EXTREMELY ANNOYING. THEIR HABIT OF DROPPING EXPLODING ACORNS ON YOUR HEAD GETS OLD REALLY FAST. PICK THEM OFF WHEN THE OPPORTUNITY ARISES.

DON'T, HOWEVER, WASTE TOO MUCH STRENGTH OF WILL FIRING AT DISTANT LADYBUGS. THROWING YOUR BLADE IS VERY EFFECTIVE AND DOESN'T USE UP ANY STRENGTH OF WILL, BUT GETTING THE TIMING DOWN IS DIFFICULT.

Continue up the path, pause at the next jump, and wait for the next rock.

The nearer you are to the top, the faster the rocks fall.

Cross the waterfall again. At the next gap, drop down to a small ledge below you.

That platform's a long way down. Jump bravely.

Jump up to the next ledge and turn around for the final leg up to the head of the falls.

Leap to the pathway and pull up to the final ledge.

Be ready to fight the first Army Ant Soldier you see, but don't move too far from the ledge. You don't want to face a gang of these bugs.

Stomp on the other two Army Ants and begin following the stream.

New Foe: Army Ant Soldier

ARMY ANT SOLDIER

THESE LOW-RANKED ARMY ANTS ARE POWERFUL FIGHTERS. FROM A DISTANCE, THEY FIRE SLOW MOVING BUT PAINFUL MUSKET SHOTS. IN CLOSE COMBAT, THEY STAB WITH THEIR BAYONETS AND HURL THEIR HAPLESS VICTIMS OVER THEIR HEADS. THEY ALSO SNAP AND SLASH WITH THEIR PINCERS.

USE YOUR CARDS AND MALLET (ALTERNATE MODE) AGAINST THE ARMY ANTS. FIGHT FROM A MIDDLE DISTANCE TO AVOID THE BAYONETS AND PINCERS—ONCE YOU'RE IN THAT CLOSE, THERE'S NO DEFENSE AGAINST THEM.

The Pool

The stream opens on a lovely pool (a puddle in reality). A statue of a weeping girl looks *very* familiar.

Approach the Mock Turtle on the right shore. He appears a bit, well, naked.

Your conversation results in a deal: If you retrieve his stolen shell from the Duchess, he'll tell you where to find Caterpillar.

WHAT'S ALL THIS THEN? DID SOMEONE DIE? HAVE YOU LOST YOUR FAMILY?

The Mock Turtle knows where you need to go next, but first you've got to get him something to cover those <u>tighty-whities</u>!

The Turtle begins floating away on a leaf. Fortunately, another leaf drops down for you. Hop on for a ride down the river.

Your chariot awaits. Jump on to begin the ride.

The River

The leaf floats at its own pace and direction down the river.

Ride down a pair of small waterfalls. As the leaf floats under some hazardous tree roots, jump onto the roots and back down to the moving leaf.

Jump up onto the low roots and rejoin your boat on the other side.

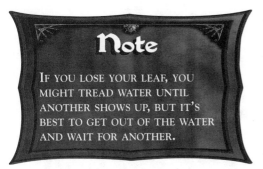

Note

IF YOU LOSE YOUR LEAF, YOU MIGHT TREAD WATER UNTIL ANOTHER SHOWS UP, BUT IT'S BEST TO GET OUT OF THE WATER AND WAIT FOR ANOTHER.

Watch the sky for dive-bombing Ladybugs.

Drop down another minor waterfall.

You see the Mock Turtle drifting in front of you just before you fall down a larger waterfall. Don't panic and you should have no trouble staying aboard.

Follow the Mock Turtle down a larger waterfall. After you reach the bottom, get to dry land and take cover.

The River, Part 2

Immediately jump to the shoreline, take cover behind a rock, and battle with a pair of Army Ant Soldiers.

Use the cover of these rocks to fight the Ants.

Jump onto the lily pads to reach another leaf, which takes you farther down the river.

Another leaf is ready to take you farther. Don't go in the water—use the lily pads.

Tip
DON'T FALL IN THE RIVER OR YOU'LL BE FOOD FOR SNARKS.

New Foe: Snark

SNARK

SNARKS ARE CURIOUS WATER DWELLERS. WHEN YOU'RE IN THE WATER, THEY BITE WITH NASTY TEETH. YOU AREN'T ALWAYS SAFE ON LAND, HOWEVER. THEY HAVE THE ABILITY TO SPIT PAINFUL GREEN GOO, WHICH HARMS YOU FROM A DISTANCE. MOST DANGEROUS IS THEIR TONGUE-LASHING ATTACK, WHICH DRAGS YOU FROM THE SAFETY OF LAND TO THEIR WATERY HOME TURF.

THEY ARE VERY FAST, BUT FORTUNATELY, THEY ARE NOT HARD TO KILL.

Jump to avoid getting kneecapped by this root.

Just after a small waterfall, jump over a tree root that threatens to knock you off your boat.

After grabbing the Meta-Essence, rejoin your leaf as it comes round the bend.

The ride takes you through a log-tunnel. After you emerge, hop on land to the right. Snap up a large Meta-Essence Crystal and jump back on the leaf when it turns the corner.

Keep your eyes on the left shore. A Blood Rose sprouts from the bank and hurls its deadly thorns. Instead of trying to battle the killer bloom, focus on avoiding shots and staying on your leaf. You won't be in the line of fire for very long.

New Foe: Blood Rose

BLOOD ROSE

THE BLOOD ROSE RISES SUDDENLY FROM THE UNDERBRUSH AND ATTACKS WITHOUT MERCY. ITS SHARP THORNS HURTLE THROUGH THE AIR IN BUNCHES. THE THORNS ARE SLOW BUT NOT EASY TO AVOID.

A FLURRY OF CARDS IS A POTENT COUNTER-ATTACK.

The Big Waterfalls

After avoiding the Rose, you approach a very large waterfall.

Just before you plummet, jump to the shore on the right.

Drop to a ledge below and leap to a lily pad floating in the pool under the waterfall.

Instead of diving over the falls, bound onto the safety of this hill.

Watch out for the pointy bits that protrude from these roots.

The pad takes you under several tree roots. Adjust your position on the lily pad to avoid being knocked off by thorns on the roots. If they knock you off, you're Snark food. Stay to the left for the first root, right for the second, and left for the third.

Go down a very small waterfall. The lily pad begins to move very erratically, so stay to the right as you go under the next root.

Jump onto the low roots stretching across the river and jump back onto the pad as it emerges from the other side.

Drop down a small waterfall and look for the Mock Turtle passing on a bridge overhead.

You know the drill by now. Climb the roots and get back on the boat.

This is your cue to prepare for a big moment. As you pass under the bridge, the river drops into a treacherous water-fall. Jump quickly!

When you see this, prepare to jump.

The vine is your best hope; jump at it as soon as it comes into view.

Leap forward to the vine hanging just beyond the crest of the falls.

Shimmy up the vine a bit, get it swinging, and jump to solid ground next to the river.

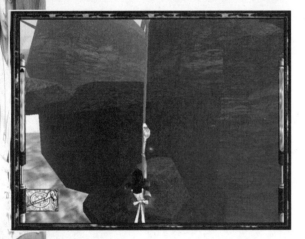

Jump here to safety, but get the rope swinging first.

Dry Land

Run down the path to arrive at a small pool. The Turtle is leaving on another leaf. Your ride drifts in soon enough.

Board the leaf.

You drift under a series of large overhanging mushrooms. Stay in the middle of the leaf and you have no trouble staying dry.

You plunge down a gigantic waterfall, but land safely.

Hollow Hideaway

The Base of the Falls

Stroll carefully down the path until a pair of Army Ant Soldiers appears in the misty distance. Waste the bugs and continue along the river.

After the shoreline path curves to the right, spar with two more Army Ant Soldiers.

Use the lily pads to get to the large tree root in the distance.

Use the two lily pads on the left to cross the water to a large tree root jutting into the river. Walk along the root to the shore.

When you can't go any farther (darn blades of grass!), turn left and walk on another peninsular tree root.

Go down the next root to get on a new leaf.

Warning

THOUGH THE WATER IS SHALLOW, YOU CAN'T GET ANYWHERE IN THIS AREA BY SWIMMING.

IF YOU SPEND MORE THAN A FEW SECONDS IN THE WATER, A GIANT FISH WILL DEVOUR YOU IN ONE BITE. YOU'VE BEEN WARNED.

The River, Part 3

Drop onto a leaf for another river run. The current takes you under another series of tree roots. Again, you'll need to shift position to stay afloat—right, left, right.

Eventually, the current "docks" your leaf at the left shoreline. You're only option is to go ashore.

Head left along the river, jump onto a lily pad, and back to the shoreline until it slopes uphill.

That big Meta-Essence may look attractive, but it's a trap. Nevermind the two Army Ant Soldiers up the hill. Your first concern is the creature guarding the prize. Yes, the Mushroom.

*An Evil Mushroom protects the Meta-Essence.
You'll need to work carefully. Perhaps
a roll of the Demon Dice!*

New Foe: Evil Mushroom

EVIL MUSHROOM

SOME MUSHROOMS MAKE YOU GROW, SOME MAKE YOU SHRINK. OTHERS SUCK YOU IN AND GRIND YOU UP WITH THEIR BIG, NASTY, POINTY TEETH. LEARN TO RECOGNIZE THESE STEALTH ENEMIES; THEY DO TREMENDOUS DAMAGE IF THEY GET THE DROP ON YOU.

THE EVIL MUSHROOM SPEWS TOXIC SPORE GAS THAT DAMAGES ANYTHING IN RANGE. IT CAN ALSO DRAW YOU IN AND LOCK ONTO YOU, CHOMPING UNTIL IT'S HAD ITS FILL.

THE CATCH IS, YOU CAN'T HURT IT UNTIL YOU GET CLOSE ENOUGH TO WAKE IT UP. SPRINT IN TO ATTRACT ITS ATTENTION, THEN RETREAT TO FIGHT FROM SAFETY.

Start by tossing Demon Dice up the hill to attract the attention of the Army Ant Soldiers. While the Demon does his work, hang back at the shoreline and back him up.

When the Ants are dead, quickly but carefully approach the Evil Mushroom. Do so before the Demon disappears. If he's still around, he immediately attacks the Mushroom. Again, provide support until the Mushroom shrivels and dies. Snap up the large Meta-Essence.

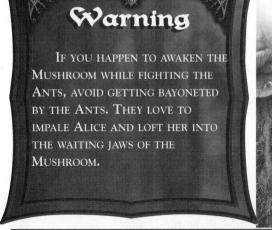

Warning

IF YOU HAPPEN TO AWAKEN THE MUSHROOM WHILE FIGHTING THE ANTS, AVOID GETTING BAYONETED BY THE ANTS. THEY LOVE TO IMPALE ALICE AND LOFT HER INTO THE WAITING JAWS OF THE MUSHROOM.

Duck, Alice, duck! Fighting Blood Roses is thorny business.

If you're lucky, the Demon then goes to work on the nearby Blood Rose. If not, let the flower spring to life and then use cover to snipe it into oblivion.

New Foe: Army Ant Commander

ARMY ANT COMMANDER

THE OFFICER CORPS OF THE ARMY ANTS IS TRULY NASTY. THOUGH THEY DON'T CARRY THE MUSKETS FAVORED BY THEIR UNDERLINGS, COMMANDERS HAVE RAZOR SHARP CUTLASSES AND CRUSHING PINCERS. THEY ALSO THROW DEVASTATING GRENADES.

USE EXTREME CAUTION WHEN FIGHTING IN CLOSE RANGE; TRY TO FOCUS ON VERY MOBILE, LONG-RANGE COMBAT.

Farther along the path, several Army Ant Soldiers are backed up by an imposing Army Ant Commander.

Continue up the hill and confront another Army Ant Solider and a Blood Rose.

Near the Rose, look down and jump on the leaf.

Ride the leaf until you see an Army Ant encampment it by burning torches.

Wait until the leaf drifts near a tree root, jump onto it, and use it to get to shore.

Tip

BEWARE THE SQUADRON OF LADYBUGS OVERHEAD.

Go past the torches and jump onto this root for the safest route to dry land.

Mow down two Army Ants guarding the bizarre house and approach the front door.

The Duchess's house; approach with great caution.

You're greeted by the chameleon, Bill McGill (a.k.a. Larry). It appears you've arrived at the house of the Duchess. Larry gleefully offers to help.

As you walk past the door, however, you find yourself sucked inside.

Just Desserts

Walk down the dark hall to the Duchess's chamber.

In the chamber, note several Meta-Essence Crystals that line the walls. Save them for your fight with the Duchess.

When you're ready to fight, hop up on the table in the middle of the room and claim the Jackbomb, which summons the Duchess.

The coveted Jackbomb sits on this table. Don't take it until you're ready to fight the Duchess.

New Toy: Jackbomb

JACKBOMB

THE JACKBOMB IS A GIDDY LITTLE DEATH MACHINE. THROW IT TO LET LOOSE A TIME-DELAYED EXPLOSION.

EVEN MORE POWERFUL IS THE ALTERNATE MODE. AFTER THE JACKBOMB LANDS, IT SPRAYS FIRE IN ALL DIRECTIONS AND TOASTS YOUR ENEMIES.

The Duchess is a voracious eater and very, very quick. Defeating her, however, is relatively easy:

♣ If she gets close to you, the Duchess often strikes with her pepper grinder club.

♣ If you hold still too long, the Duchess picks you up and chews on your head before tossing you into the nearest wall. Ouch.

♣ From middle distances, watch out for a spray from the Duchess's pepper grinder.

♣ Projectiles are useless against her. She instantly breaks into a blinding run after you launch the attack.

♣ Watch her left hand. When it glows blue, she's summoning the pig-baby grenade. Run as she tosses.

♣ Make quick work of the preoccupied Duchess by hurling the newly-acquired Jackbomb. The alternate attack is especially effective. It only takes a few hits to finish the job.

Mmmmmmm, Alice-head!

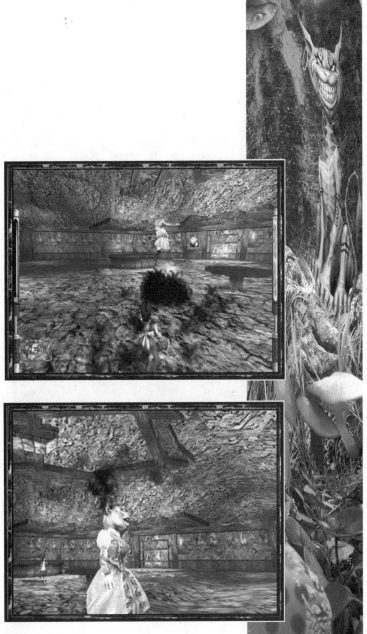

Watch out for the pepper spray.

After your victory, Larry and the Mock Turtle congratulate you and lead you on a swim to the Wonderland Woods.

Gesundheit! Sweet victory.

Wholly Morel Ground

You begin underwater. The Mock Turtle gets you safely to dry land, but you must stay in his bubble trail at all times. If you lose him, your air supply only lasts a few moments before you drown.

Stay close to the bubbles.

Various hazards await you in these underground caverns: Stalactites fall from the ceiling. When you see them start to fall, pause briefly and let them pass before you proceed.

Chunks of the ceiling have a tendency to drop away just as you swim near them. Pause and let them fall before catching up to the Turtle.

The sky is falling. Best to let these ceiling tiles and stalactites fall before you try to pass.

Giant clams open tantalizingly and snap closed. Some contain Meta-Essence Crystals; wait for them to close and open again and then swim through to claim the prize.

Giant clams hold treasures richer than pearls but claiming your loot is dangerous

Beware of the air jets on the cave floor. They push you into the sharp stalactites on the ceiling if you swim over them.

Snarks are also a big problem. Pause to fight them, but keep track of your guide. The Blade or Cards are your best bets.

These jets lift you right into the spikes above.

Note

YOU DON'T HAVE TO FOLLOW THE TURTLE'S EVERY MOVE. IN FACT, IT'S SOMETIMES VERY UNWISE TO DO SO. WHAT'S IMPORTANT, HOWEVER, IS THAT YOU NEVER LET HIM OUT OF YOUR SIGHT AND STAY AS MUCH AS POSSIBLE IN HIS WAKE. IF YOU LOSE HIM MOMENTARILY, TRY TO CATCH UP BY CUTTING A CORNER ON HIS ROUTE.

Swim toward the friendly creature and settle in among his bubbles to begin.

The journey begins with a trip through the first few caverns. Stay close to the Turtle during this first phase and be mindful of obstacles.

The Temple

Continue following the Mock Turtle until you come to the doorway of an ancient temple. Things get a bit trickier now.

As you enter the temple, you get your first real taste of Snarks. Or, more to the point, they get their first taste of you.

In this area, beware of giant clams, falling ceiling tiles, and falling columns.

The temple entrance

Sarcophagus Room

Next, go through a portal to a large chamber with a sarcophagus on the ceiling. Pause to let the falling columns drop in front of you.

The sarcophagus room

Giant Fish Room

Pass through the next portal and dive straight down to follow the Turtle. He brings you to very large room populated by Snarks.

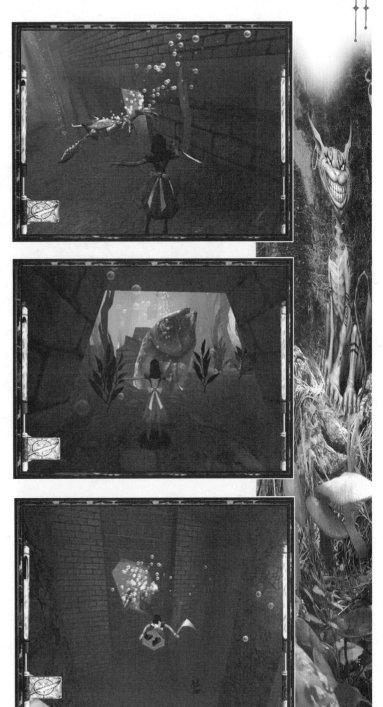

Dive downward to get to the next area.

After you enter the room, pause. A gigantic fish pops up from the floor in front of you. Wait for it to retract and swim on safely.

The Mock Turtle takes a dangerous and circuitous route through this room; stay with him, but don't follow him everywhere.

Pause in the portal to avoid becoming part of the food chain.

When it seems you can go no farther, the Mock Turtle bowls his way through the wall. Follow him through the hole he's made and your swim is complete.

The makeshift exit is good enough.

Chapter 7
Wonderland Woods

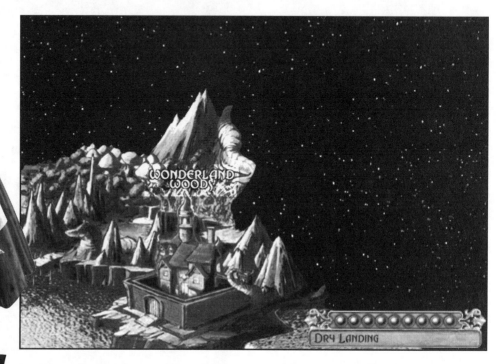

In this region of Wonderland you'll meet:

Friends:
- ♣ White Rabbit
- ♣ Caterpillar
- ♣ Oracle

Foes:
- ♣ Ladybug
- ♣ Army Ant Solider
- ♣ Blood Rose
- ♣ Snark
- ♣ Army Ant Sergeant
- ♣ Ant Lion
- ♣ Centipede (Boss)

- ♣ Fire Imp
- ♣ Magma Man
- ♣ Phantasmagoria
- ♣ Boojum
- ♣ Diamond Card Guard
- ♣ Club Card Guard
- ♣ Red Pawn

To boost your budding arsenal of deadly Toys, you'll find:

♣ Ice Wand

♣ Demon Dice (second)

Dry Landing

At the Pool

Turn slightly to the left and walk along the water's edge.

Pummel the Army Ant Soldiers around the bend. Check out the two high ledges for Meta-Essence Crystals.

After the Turtle leaves, head off to the left. Those crystals might be useful after the first fight.

Tip

LADYBUGS ARE A CONSTANT THREAT IN THESE LEVELS. KEEP YOUR EARS OPEN AND WATCH THE SKIES. STOP DURING PEACEFUL MOMENTS TO THIN OUT THE SWARMS.

This pond is home to Snarks and, on the far shore, an Army Ant Soldier.

Continue to a lovely pond. Before diving in, however, do away with the Ladybug buzzing overhead and the Army Ant Soldier across the pool to the left.

The pond is full of Snarks. Just because you're on the shore, don't think you're safe—their tongues can pull you into a watery grave.

Jump quickly between the two lily pads and onto the vine. Turn around and swing to the hill to the left.

Scale the hill toward a waterfall and prepare for a Blood Rose to pop up on across the water.

Get on this vine and swing to the hill to the left.

Waterfall

Go around the waterfall.

There's a series of ledges that appear to be the way to go, but the final ledge is simply too high.

That's not the way up. It's too high.

Instead of climbing, jump on the glowing mushroom near the ledge. After it bounces you high in the air, turn around and grab the vine.

Climb the vine and swing to the ledge to meet with Rabbit.

The glowing mushrooms have a springboard effect. Jump on them to reach great heights.

Turn in the air to grab this vine, then swing to join Rabbit.

Catching Rabbit

Those moss shelves provide stable footing.

Follow Rabbit to the cliff ahead and jump down to the moss ledges on the giant tree ahead. Drop down to the second moss ledge. Toss a few Toys at the Army Ant Soldier standing on the distant ledge.

Leap for the vine and swing to the ledge.

Trudge down the passage and pluck the Blood Rose.

Don't fall off this hill or you'll be back where you started.

In the clearing (which looks down on the beginning of this level), spar with another Blood Rose and an Army Ant Soldier to get the Meta-Essence Crystal on the high ledge.

Further up the passage, liquidate an Army Ant Commander and the squadron of Ladybugs overhead.

Big Drop

The next step is a *very* long way down. You can simply jump down, but it costs you some Sanity. Instead, look straight over the ledge to see a glowing mushroom below. The glowing mushrooms help you bounce.

Take a chance and fall to the glowing mushroom below.

Drop straight down onto it and bound to the next glowing mushroom, then up onto the next-lowest ledge.

Pulverize the Blood Rose and the Army Ant Solider guarding the lowest ledge.

Plummet down to the glowing mushrooms again and grab the first of two vines.

Swing to the second vine, then to the ledge.

*Go from the mushrooms to the vine
to get out of this mess.*

Inside the Hollow Tree

Head inside the hollow tree, pausing to deal with the Blood Rose, and climb up the short ramp.

This glowing mushroom has enough spring to launch you to almost any of the ledges in the hollow tree.

Jump on the vine and climb to near the top.

Swing and jump to the glowing mushroom and up to the lower of two ledges.

Drop back down to the glowing mushroom and lob yourself up to the higher of the two ledges. Grab the Rage Box.

Use the mushroom again to reach the large ledge and the exit.

The Rage Box helps you get through the traffic that awaits outside the tree.

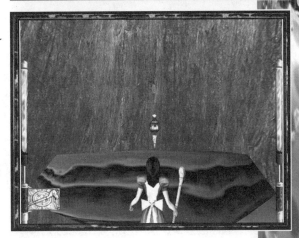

Outside the Hollow Tree

Plow through the Army Any Soldier, the Blood Rose, and the Army Ant Commander.

At a T-intersection, go left. Clobbering an Army Ant Soldier, you arrive at a chasm spanned by a long bridge.

The Bridge

Unfortunately, just as you arrive, the bridge collapses. Use the glowing mushrooms on the right to traverse the canyon.

These mushrooms make crossing the canyon a very wild ride.

Turn left to ward off a Blood Rose. If you haven't already retrieved the Jackbomb, another one is just a few jumps away on the Blood Rose's ledge. Watch out for the Evil Mushroom, though.

Resume the trail as it climbs uphill.

The Great Tree

Start by jumping to the vine hanging between you and the Great Tree.

Swing over to the Great Tree and start walking around it counterclockwise.

Swing to the first moss ledge, drop to the second, then leap to the next vine.

Climb up to near the top of the vine. Swoop down to the ledge and decapitate the Army Ant Commander.

Look out below! Be ready to fight when you land.

The Stream

A small hill takes to you a rushing stream. First, bury the Blood Roses, then walk across the rocks to reach the left shoreline near the waterfall.

Cross the stream by dancing on the rocks. Watch out for Snarks!

Warning

THIS STREAM IS FULL OF SNARKS. MOVE FAST ON THIS CROSSING TO AVOID THEIR SALVOS OF GREEN GOO.

Herbaceous Border

Clearing of Death

Walk forward to a clearing and meet with Rabbit.

Unfortunately, Rabbit meets his untimely end under the foot of a mysterious passer-by. Alice, now without a guide, despairs. You have no choice but to go on.

The clearing leads to three paths. The first, marked by a gigantic tiger lily, is where you just came from.

The second is marked by a large sunflower and is the most difficult route.

The path marked by the mushroom is the way to begin.

The third, marked by a giant mushroom is the best place to start. Stroll up the path, destroy the Blood Rose, and jump into the hole in the ground.

Dive into this hole.

Steam Room

Follow a long tunnel to a chamber with two large steam vents. Jump to the first, float to the second, and land gently on the distant ledge.

Ride the steam to the other side.

Continue to a Y-intersection (marked by a green light). Go left.

Mallet Chamber

As you approach the Mallet Chamber, those giant feet interfere again, causing a bridge to collapse.

Hurtle off the mushroom to the bridge above you.

Use the glowing mushroom below you to reach the bridge above.

Cross the bridge toward the glowing Croquet Mallet and pass through the portal.

Exit this chamber near the Croquet Mallet.

Island Room

This room features an elevated, isolated platform in the middle of the area below. Ignore it; you're just passing through.

Cross the long winding bridge to a doorway, then enter the tunnel.

Cut across this twisty bridge.

Card Chamber

This room is highlighted by a ring-shaped bridge below. A steam vent rises from it.

The steam vent in this room takes you to the vines.

Jump onto the steam vent and ride it to the first vine. Scale the rope, then leap to the next vine.

Hop up the ledges to reach the passage to the surface.

Leap to the rock ledge and over to another ledge holding Cards. Climb the ramp, then pull yourself up to the surface.

The Surface

Immediately spin around and duel with the Blood Rose.

Turn left and move down the path to fight another Blood Rose.

After you can go no farther, turn right and jump to a vine. Swing down to the ground *to the left* of the tree's large root.

It's time to swing again.

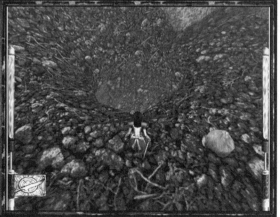

Drop down the hole and follow the tunnel.

Go down another hole to leave this dangerous place.

Rolling Stones

Uh-oh! The Ladybugs are really torqued. They drop a giant marble into the tunnel you've just entered. *Run!*

The Spiral Tunnel

Keep running down the long winding shaft. Stay to the inside of the curve.

Don't stop for anything. You want as big a lead as possible after you get to the end of this chase.

Hurtle through a portal and continue running down the tunnel.

Mushroom Chamber

Hold to the path until it abruptly ends. Leap to the glowing mushroom to the right.

Boing …

You land on a solid platform, but don't pause.

Immediately jump to the next glowing mushroom, onto the ledge, and continue through the tunnel.

… Boing!

Bone Bridge

Run across the twisty bridge of bones.

Watch your step on this narrow trestle. Go through the portal and continue through the tunnel.

Thank heaven for fossils.

Ice Room

Don't look back as you cross the large ice field in this room. After the rock arrives, its weight causes the ice behind you to crack.

You want to be as far across this ice field as possible when the rock arrives.

As long as you don't stop running, you won't lose your footing or fall into the fast-approaching cracked ice.

Stroll down the slippery tunnel. After the ground drops out beneath your feet, relax and wait to land.

Icy Reception

Slide carefully down the icy tunnel.

Ice Wand Cavern

After the tunnel opens into a vast cavern, head to the right.

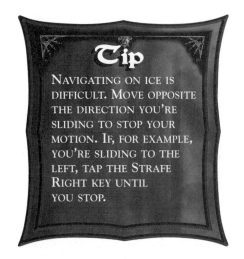

Tip

NAVIGATING ON ICE IS DIFFICULT. MOVE OPPOSITE THE DIRECTION YOU'RE SLIDING TO STOP YOUR MOTION. IF, FOR EXAMPLE, YOU'RE SLIDING TO THE LEFT, TAP THE STRAFE RIGHT KEY UNTIL YOU STOP.

Take the path to the right.

Climb the ice ledges. As you come to the top, you spot a new Toy glowing on a nearby platform: the Ice Wand.

Up ahead in the distance is a shimmering light. It's the Ice Wand.

New Toy: Ice Wand

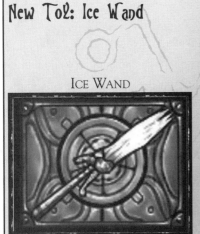

ICE WAND

THE ICE WAND IS A CHILLY BUT EXPENSIVE WEAPON. IN PRIMARY FIRE MODE, THE WAND SPRAYS A BLAST OF FREEZING AIR FOR AS LONG AS YOU HOLD THE MOUSE BUTTON. AFTER THE TARGET IS SUFFICIENTLY DAMAGED, HE OR SHE FREEZES AND EVENTUALLY EXPIRES. THE ONLY HITCH IS THAT THE WAND USES UP A LOT OF STRENGTH OF WILL.

ALTERNATE FIRE OFFERS A VERY USEFUL DEFENSIVE ABILITY. IN EXCHANGE FOR A REASONABLY SMALL AMOUNT OF STRENGTH OF WILL, YOU AUTOMATICALLY BUILD A PROTECTIVE ICE WALL. YOU CAN BUILD SEVERAL OF THESE IF CIRCUMSTANCES REQUIRE ADDED DEFENSE.

Drop down to the small ledge below. Don't slide off as you land; this jump is tricky.

Turn and leap to the platform holding the Ice Wand.

As you land, falling rocks destroy the bridge to the exit.

You get the Ice Wand but lose the bridge. Oh well, no problem.

Jump back to the small ledge and over to the exit.

Jump back the way you came and onto the exit ledge.

Rolling Stones Again

As you start down the passage, it's time to run again. That gigantic marble is hot on your tail.

Run as hard as you can and be very careful of the slippery ice.

About halfway down, rocks fall in front of you. Pause to avoid running under them. Chase these new rocks down the tunnel. The rocks burst through the seeming dead end of this tunnel, providing you with an exit.

*More rocks fall in front of you.
Don't worry; these are helpful
as long as you don't run into them.*

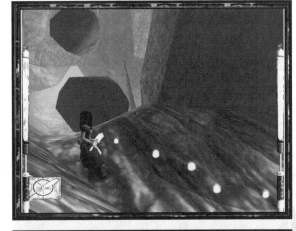

Daylight

As you emerge, immediately sidestep
away from the tunnel's exit until the
pursuing rock passes by. Pass the time by
sniping at Ladybugs.

Go right along the rocky ledge.

*After you see sunlight again, scoot to the right
to get out of harm's way.*

Caterpillar

After you reach the end, turn to face the
twin steam vents in the cavern. Your destination is the very high ledge on the
other side of the cavern.

Jump onto the first vent and, as soon
as possible, move to the second vent.

Move between the steam vents.

Let the second vent carry you as high as possible before trying for the ledge.

View Alice from above and keep her centered on the vent until she reaches sufficient height to leap to the high ledge.

Walk up the pathway to meet Caterpillar.

Ah, Caterpillar, we meet again.

Fungiferous Flora

The Mushroom Room

Before you move a muscle, take stock of what's around you. There's no way to go forward without waking up at least one of those Evil Mushrooms.

Creep forward and activate the middle Mushroom. Back off and lob a Jackbomb or two.

Sneak past the fourth Mushroom guarding the corridor.

At the other end of the corridor, eliminate the next Mushroom before you venture out.

Mushrooms everywhere!

Keep your distance to avoid waking up many of the Evil Mushrooms.

The Ant Ravine

After you emerge, quickly eliminate two Army Ant Soldiers. Prepare for a new enemy: the Ant Lion.

New Foe: Ant Lion

ANT LION

THE ANT LION IS A VICIOUS, MINDLESS BEAST. MINDLESS, BUT SNEAKY. WATCH OUT FOR ITS PAINFUL PINCER ATTACK, BITE, AND TAIL WHIP. TO MAKE MATTERS WORSE, IT CAN BURROW INTO THE GROUND WITH BLINDING SPEED. WITHOUT WARNING, IT SPRINGS FROM THE GROUND, LUNGING AT YOUR SOFT THROAT. VICIOUS.

IT'S EASY, BY THE WAY, TO THINK THAT THE ANT LION IS DEAD WHEN IT'S JUST UNDERGROUND. REMEMBER: IT ISN'T DEAD UNTIL IT RELEASES ITS META-ESSENCE.

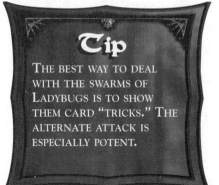

March forward, obliterating another
Evil Mushroom and a Blood Rose. Around
the bend, eradicate two more Mushrooms
and three Army Ant Soldiers.

Puddle Diving

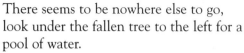

There seems to be nowhere else to go,
look under the fallen tree to the left for a
pool of water.

Do something about those Snarks,
then dive in and swim under the tree.

Look down to find the pool on the left.

*You have to fight your
way out of the water.*

After you surface,
destroy an Evil Mushroom.

Headquarters Approach

Scale the hill to your right after you come out of the pool. Lay claim to the second Demon Dice, located in an alcove.

The second of three Demon Dice is up this hill.

New Toy: Demon Dice 2

DEMON DICE

POSSESSING TWO DEMON DICE ENABLES YOU TO SUMMON AN EVEN STRONGER DEMON: THE SERPENT DEMON.

Army Ant Base

Jump in the knothole in the tree. Drop down the into the Centipede's main base. The Army Ants approach to do their master's bidding. The battle, however, only lasts a moment as you're quickly overwhelmed.

This knothole leads to the Centipede's headquarters.

Centipede's Sanctum

The Soldiers shove Alice into the Centipede's headquarters. Your only option is to fight and claim the Mushroom you need to grow large.

The Centipede's armor is nearly impervious to attack. A large red spot on his underbelly is unprotected. Attack there; anything else is a waste of Strength of Will.

The large red spot on the Centipede's underbelly is the only place he takes damage.

Snap and throw. Don't stand still or this is what you'll see.

The crawlers are a constant menace but also a source of Meta-Essence.

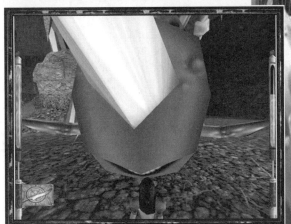

When the Centipede uses his head, he really uses his head.

Winning the right to bite the Mushroom is no simple task. The Centipede has several attacks:

♣ He spits green goo.

♣ He expels crawlers that latch onto and bite you. They're easy to kill but can't be loosened after they attach. Eventually they die on their own.

♣ He rams with his spike helmet.

♣ He grabs with his pincers and tosses you across the room. Often this lands you in the abyss surrounding the arena.

♣ He uses his sharpened legs to stab. These limbs do damage any time you come in contact with them.

Get in close, wait for the Centipede to expose his underbelly, attack, then run away to collect a Meta-Essence. Repeat.

While it sounds overwhelming, there are a few things to keep in mind:

♣ The crawlers are your main source of Meta-Essence during this fight. After they die by either your hand or nature, they leave behind precious Crystals.

♣ Get in tight, right under the Centipede's front legs and keep a medium distance—enough to avoid getting cut too badly by the front legs.

♣ Eventually, the Centipede rears up and exposes his soft underbelly. When he does, give him a full dose of the Ice Wand. The Ice Wand's range and lack of precision are its assets here.

♣ Don't stay close for too long, hoping to finish off the mighty insect in one blow. You frequently need to scour for Meta-Essence to keep up both your Sanity and Strength of Will.

♣ There's a Grasshopper Tea power-up around the periphery of the arena. It can help you jump higher and run faster.

♣ Be mindful of your position; it's possible to fall out of the arena.

Hop up the impromptu stairs to get to the magic Mushroom.

After the monster is destroyed, a circle of stalactites falls from the ceiling, forming stairs. Climb them and have a bite of Mushroom. It's time to grow up.

Caterpillar's Plot

Back at full size, it's time to get some insight.

The Canyon of Fire

This canyon has four passages, each marked with signposts:

1. The first leads to the Cave of the Oracle.
2. The second leads to the Pale Realm (you'll go there next).
3. The third goes to the Jabberwock's Lair. It's locked now.
4. The fourth goes to Queen of Hearts Land (sign: "Majestic Maze"). You won't go there until much later.

These signposts point the way.

Before you do anything, swat away the pesky Fire Imps as they converge on you.

New Foe: Fire Imp

FIRE IMP

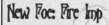

THE FIRE IMP IS A LITTLE PEST. ALL IT REALLY DOES IS POKE YOU WITH ITS PITCHFORK, BUT IT'S DANGEROUS NEVERTHELESS. WHEN IT TRAVELS IN GROUPS, WATCH OUT.

Turn right and jump over the lava river. Follow the bridge to a platform rising from the pool of fire. On it rests part of the Jabberwock Eyestaff, which you'll need.

Scale this hazardous island to get the staff section of the Jabberwock Eyestaff.

Look for a small ledge near the top. Jump onto it, then to the top to get the staff.

Return to where you began.

The Oracle's Canyon

Go through this tunnel to see the Oracle.

Go to the signpost and find your way to the "Cave of the Oracle." Take the leftmost of the three main passageways (through the stone tunnel).

On the way, you encounter your first Magma Man.

New Foe: Magma Man

MAGMA MAN

THE MAGMA MAN RISES FROM POOLS OF LAVA. WHEN HE'S STILL MOLTEN (ORANGE), HE HAS TREMENDOUS RANGE WITH HIS PUNCHES AND CAN SET YOU ON FIRE. HE ALSO SPITS FIRE. AFTER HE'S HARDENED TO ROCK, HE RELIES ALMOST ENTIRELY ON A TWO-FISTED POUND AND A JAB.

THE WIND-UP FOR THE MAGMA MAN'S PUNCHES IS VERY SLOW. USE THIS DELAY TO GET IN SOME SOLID JABS AS HE REARS BACK.

As you emerge, deal with the pair of Fire Imps and then whip around to snipe at the Diamond Card Guard on the ledge behind you.

Next, move forward to face the pair of Phantasmagorias.

New Foe: Phantasmagoria

PHANTASMAGORIA

These wraiths seem placid when at rest. Approach them, however, and they show their true faces.

Don't stand still near them or you're temporarily frozen solid by their spectral chains, which can be fired from a long distance. They also can suck away your Strength of Will.

Continue left and forward. As the path narrows, two Boojums run up to say long-time-no-see. Show them what they've missed.

As you move into a large, open cavern, the Oracle addresses you. You need to collect the remaining parts of the Jabberwock's Eyestaff. Start by visiting the Pale Realm.

Return to the main cavern. You find that new enemies have repopulated the level for your return.

The Oracle speaks in rhyme, but you should have no trouble understanding what it means.

Path to the Pale Realm

Go down the second passage (marked "Pale Realm").

After you enter the cavern, deal harshly with the Boojums.

Next up is a Red Pawn.

New Foe: Red Pawn

RED PAWN

THE RED PAWN IS THE WEAKEST OF THE RED CHESS PIECES. HIS ONLY OFFENSIVE STRIKE IS THE CHESS PIECE EQUIVALENT OF A HEAD-BUTT. HE'S SURPRISINGLY POWERFUL, HOWEVER, KNOCKING YOU BACK SEVERAL FEET AND SLICING OFF SUBSTANTIAL SANITY.

As the passage opens wider, the landscape begins to change. Chessboard ground is your first clue that the village of the white chess pieces can't be too far away.

Welcome to the land of chess pieces.
Don't fall through the board
or the game's over.

Chessboard Stairs

Climb up the chessboard stairs, cutting a path through several Red Pawns.

At the top, shoot down a Diamond Card Guard patrolling in the distance and look to your left for a Darkened Looking Glass. This allows you to get to the Pale Realm safely.

The Darkened Looking Glass allows you to get to the Pale Realm without anyone noticing.

Turn the corner to the left and jump your way to the front gate of the Pale Realm.

The route to the portal is precarious. Don't fall through the floor.

Chapter 8
Looking Glass Land

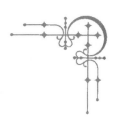

In this region of Wonderland you'll meet:

Friends
♣ White King

Foes
♣ Red Pawn
♣ Red Knight
♣ Red Bishop
♣ Red Rook
♣ Red King (Boss)

♣ Clockwork Automaton
♣ Phantasmagoria
♣ Nightmare Spiders
♣ Boojum
♣ Tweedledee and Tweedledum (Bosses)

To boost your budding arsenal of deadly Toys, you'll find:

- ♣ Jacks
- ♣ Demon Dice 3

The Pale Realm

Market Courtyard

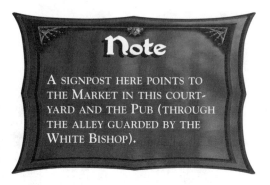

Note

A SIGNPOST HERE POINTS TO THE MARKET IN THIS COURT-YARD AND THE PUB (THROUGH THE ALLEY GUARDED BY THE WHITE BISHOP).

Chat with the White Bishop.

Move forward into the courtyard and approach the White Bishop. After a wordless conversation, you have an understanding.

He lets you use him as a disguise to get to the Pub. Remember that the Bishop can only move diagonally. Navigate this room to avoid holes in the floor and spikes from the roof.

As the Bishop, you can only move diagonally.

1. Move diagonally forward one square to the left.

2. Move diagonally forward two squares to the right.

3. Move diagonally forward three squares to the left. This brings you to the left wall.

4. Move diagonally forward two squares to the right. This brings you to another wall.

5. Move diagonally one square to the right.

6. Move diagonally one square to the left.

7. Move diagonally two squares to the right.

8. Move diagonally one square to the right.

9. Move diagonally two squares to the left. This brings you to another wall.

10. Move diagonally two squares to the left. This brings you to another wall.

11. Move diagonally one square to the left.

12. Move diagonally two squares to the right.

With that, you're restored to your non–chess piece self. Walk up the stairs.

Pub Courtyard

Enter a wide courtyard. A pedestal in the center holds a Croquet Mallet (glowing green). The courtyard is overlooked by a massive clock tower and is populated by a Red Knight and two Red Pawns.

This large courtyard is marked by this green-lit pedestal and the high clock tower.

New Foe: Red Knight

RED KNIGHT

THE RED KNIGHT ATTACKS WITH SEVERAL SWINGS OF HIS SWORD. AVOID ATTACKING HIS SHIELD SIDE; HE BLOCKS EFFECTIVELY.

Explore all the doors in this courtyard.

A large, white door near the Pub is locked and guarded by a White Rook. He's waiting for it to open.

Tip

IF YOU STILL NEED THE MALLET, CLIMB ONTO THE PEDESTAL. BE WARNED, HOWEVER, A CADRE OF RED CHESS PIECES WILL CONVERGE IF YOU TRY TO STEAL THE MALLET. IF YOU DON'T NEED THIS TOY, DON'T BOTHER.

Remember this large white door.

After you've checked all the courtyard's nooks and crannies, enter the double doors located to the right of where you first entered the courtyard.

*Look for the ornate door
for the way to go. Be careful!*

Elevator Tower

Ride the elevator up. You have a choice of two doors.

The door to the left is worth exploring, but leads nowhere. Go through the door to the right. At the end of the balcony, turn right and stop.

*Explore the door to the left,
but enter the right one.*

A series of spikes quickly poke up from the floor. Each time they rise, they move back one row on the floor. Follow the spikes until they reach the last row, then exit the hall.

Turn right.

*Study the behavior of these spikes
to cross them without injury.*

Bridge Courtyard

Duel with two Red Bishops.

Note

LOOK IN THE DISTANCE AS YOU ENTER THIS COURTYARD TO SEE A WHITE PAWN FLEEING INTO A DISTANT DOORWAY.

New Foe: Red Bishop

RED BISHOP

BEWARE THE RED BISHOP'S STAFF, WHICH HE SWINGS DURING CLOSE COMBAT. WHEN FIGHTING BEYOND STAFF RANGE, HE FIRES A VERY FAST LASER-LIKE BEAM.

THE BISHOP IS QUICK, SO USE THE ICE WAND AGAINST HIM.

Move toward the bridge and manhandle the Red Knight who leaps out from the high window as you cross. Turn right at the locked double doors. Immediately rush to defend the White Pawn against the Red Knight.

After you're done with the Red Knight, go through the ornate door to the right.

Turn right and climb the stairs. To the left is another set of stairs (with Cards floating nearby). Cut down the two Red Pawns bounding down the hall.

Go through the door to the left to a balcony overlooking the Pub courtyard. Pull the switch. This opens the white door near the Pub.

Pull on this switch to open the large white doors in the Pub courtyard.

Pub Courtyard

Return to the Pub courtyard and follow the White Rook through the now-open door. A Red Knight lurks in the alcove next to the door.

Turn left as you go through the door and descend the stairs. Help the White Rook fend off an attack from the Red Bishop.

Backtrack to the stairs and climb up to the ledge to the left. Pick up the Super Meta-Essence and rush into the water wheel courtyard.

Water Wheel Courtyard

Slice up the Red Knight, Red Bishop, and the Red Rook.

New Foe: Red Rook

RED ROOK

THE RED ROOK IS A BRUTE, PLAIN AND SIMPLE. STAY TO HIS SIDE, BEHIND HIM, OR OUT OF ARM'S REACH TO AVOID HIS CRUSHING JAB PUNCH. IF YOU STAY TOO FAR AWAY, HE RUSHES FORWARD WITH HIS HEAD DOWN AND FISTS OUT.

Explore the area but don't head into the water yet. Turn left after the bridge. Turn left to find another large white door. Two Red Pawns sneak up from behind as you approach.

After the door drops, meet a White Knight. Like the Bishop before him, he lets you take his guise to cross the next room.

Remember you can only move in L-patterns; avoid the spikes and holes in the floor.

Note

NEAR YOUR MEETING WITH THE WHITE KNIGHT, THERE IS A SERIES OF INACCESSIBLE STAIRS FLOATING IN SPACE. YOU'LL FIND OUT HOW TO REACH THOSE LATER.

As a Knight, you can only move in an L-pattern. Watch out for holes in the floor and ceiling spikes.

1. Move forward.

2. Move one square forward and two to the left.

3. Move two squares to the right. You'll automatically move one more to the right.

4. Move two squares straight ahead and one square to the left.

5. Turn 180 degrees and go one square straight ahead and two squares to the left.

6. Move two squares to the right and you'll automatically move one square to the right.

7. Move one square to the left and you'll automatically move two squares to the left.

8. Move to the right and you'll automatically complete the L.

You shed your knightly exterior and regain your freedom of movement. Go forward and left, up the stairs to liquidate the Red Bishop.

Up and Down Landing

From this landing, go left or right.

Detour briefly left. If you go as far as possible, you can see a ledge high above the water, marked by a large Meta-Essence Crystal. Keep this area in mind and return to the landing.

Once you've raised the water level in this village, you'll return here.

Enter the door and climb up the stairs.

Go up the stairs to the right from the landing and through the unlocked door to the right.

Rub out the two Red Pawns and climb the rickety staircase.

Upstairs, claim a Jackbomb.

Blow up this wall with a Jackbomb to find a secret stash of Meta-Essence.

Note

A Secret Area: Note the crack in the wall behind two barrels. Lob a Jackbomb toward it and take cover. The bomb opens a hole in the wall. Follow the steps to a large Sanity Shard. After you're through, return to the upstairs area with the hole in the wall.

Water Wheel Courtyard, Upper Level

Pass through this door to get to the bridges above the courtyard.

Go through the door to a high balcony. Turn the Red Knight around the corner into glue and follow the wooden walkway to the first tower.

Turn right and cross the walkway to the second tower. Eliminate the two Red Pawns and pull the switch.

The switch starts the water wheel that raises the water level throughout the village.

Retrace your steps to the Up and Down Landing.

Pull the switch in the towers to raise the village's water level.

Up and Down Landing, Again

After you arrive at the landing, continue down the stairs straight ahead.

Turn left and continue until you can't go any farther.

Dive into the water and swim to the ledge with the large Meta-Essence Crystal.

With the higher water level, you can easily swim to the ledge holding the large Meta-Essence Crystal.

Tip

SWIM AROUND THE VILLAGE AND CHECK OUT THE AREA BEHIND THE WATER WHEEL.

Turn right immediately and gun down two Red Pawns. Go up the ramp and turn left through the double doors. Proceed through the archway and turn right.

Pull up and get ready to fight.

Castling

The Town Square

Turn right and head through the double doors into a vast courtyard.

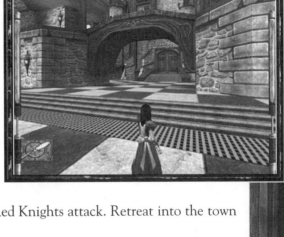

Duck under this archway.

Go under the bridge to the right and witness a terrible scene: The White Queen is carted away by a pair of Red Rooks while two Red Knights stand guard.

After the Queen is spirited away, the Red Knights attack. Retreat into the town square and destroy both Knights.

Explore the bridge up the stairs, then enter the castle doors.

The Castle Foyer

Throw open the next double doors to interrupt a wild fight between White and Red chess pieces. Intervene on the side of the White.

A battle rages. You can help or simply move around the fray.

Look for a door on the right side of the room marked by portraits of Alice and the Cheshire Cat. Go through the door nearby.

Go right and slap down two Red Knights. Turn right through a tall door.

Look for this pair of portraits and go through the adjacent door. There's a Rage Box behind the Cat's picture. Approach the portrait to collect the Box.

The Portrait Gallery

Lend a hand in the raging battle if you wish.

Another fight is under way.

Climb up the stairs and turn left at the landing.

Go through the double doors atop the stairs.

Go upstairs and through the doors to the throne room of the White King.

Throne Room

Walk across the room to meet with the White King. He asks you to liberate the White Queen. He assigns a single Pawn to help you.

Follow either of the two White Rooks to find the way to the Red Realm. Destroy any opposition along the way if the Rook doesn't take care of it himself.

Follow the White Rook to the portal to the Red Realm.

The Rook leads you to a portal. Jump through it.

Jump through the portal.

Checkmate in Red

The Red Realm should look very familiar, albeit a bit more colorful. The layout is the same as the Pale Realm, but your tasks are not.

Red Water Wheel Courtyard

Step forward out of the alcove and drop down to the floor to pick off a couple of Red Pawns.

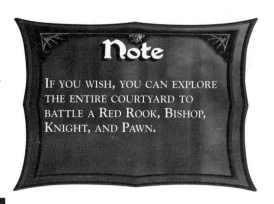

Note

IF YOU WISH, YOU CAN EXPLORE THE ENTIRE COURTYARD TO BATTLE A RED ROOK, BISHOP, KNIGHT, AND PAWN.

Dive in the ruddy water.

Descend the stairs and jump into the water left of the bridge.

Turn around and swim toward the gap in the wall.

Jump to grab the rope and climb to the top of the tower.

Look for this gap and swim to find the rope.

Climb the rope to the top of the tower. Enemies await.

Red Water Wheel Courtyard, Upper Level

Cross the bridge to the next tower and turn left. Slaughter the Red Pawns on the next bridge.

Head into the only available door and then through a few more. Starting to sound like Caterpillar, eh?

Enter the red door. Pick up the third Demon Die.

New Tol: Demon Dice 3

DEMON DICE 3

THE THIRD DEMON DIE ADDS ANOTHER MIGHTY MINION OF HELL TO YOUR REPERTOIRE: THE WINGED DEMON LORD.

Go through two more red doors and look out of the window to see the White Queen executed. You're too late.

Continue down the hall as it twists and turns. A Bishop and two Knights attempt to halt your revenge mission. Ascend a short staircase and turn right. Carefully contend with two Red Rooks (on the ground) and one Red Bishop (above).

Descend a short staircase, turn right, and go up another short one.

These doors lead to the Red King's lair. Be ready to fight.

Turn left to enter the ornate double doors.

Fall down the hole.

At the end of the passageway, drop into the hole in the floor. Walk out to the drawbridge to fight the Red King.

The Red King

The Red King has all the powers of his minions plus several others.

The simple scepter swing is quite painful.

*Like certain Card Guards,
the Red King tosses killer diamond projectiles.*

*His evil energy beams are almost
impossible to avoid.*

♣ He strikes with all the force of a Rook with his scepter.

♣ He throws diamonds. These move much faster and track better than the Diamond Card Guard's projectiles. Jump erratically to avoid them.

♣ His Majesty fires an evil energy beam similar to the Bishop's. It's almost impossible to escape unscathed from this beam.

♣ He tosses grenades faster than you can avoid them.

The Red King is very quick, but not invulnerable. You can win a hand-to-hand battle if you have sufficient combat skill. If you can sidestep-attack quickly and erratically and strike with the Mallet, you can do quite well.

Make a habit of picking up the Meta-Essence Crystals that appear in the board's corners.

Still, there's an easier way. Use your Strength of Will to keep the Red King occupied. Throw a Jackbomb to distract the Red King's attention away from you. Then, refuel your Strength of Will as Meta-Essence Crystals appear randomly in the corners of the chessboard.

When the Red King has his hands full with Jackbombs, you can snipe from afar. The Ice Wand, may be useful here.

When the Red King perishes, you are transported to an even stranger place.

Mirror Image

Alice awakens in a *very* strange place. The entire building is turned, literally, on its side.

Scale the ledge to the right of the chandelier for a Rage Box.

First, go toward the ledge to the right of the portrait (from which the Cat spoke). Jump onto the wooden beam on the wall (ceiling). Climb up a few steps and turn around to jump to the ledge. Pick up a Rage Box.

Head into the funhouse maze through this doorway.

Note

IN THIS HALL OF MIRRORS, CLOCKWORK AUTOMATONS BURST FROM THE MIRRORED WALLS. GET THE RAGE BOX, OR YOU WON'T GET THROUGH HERE WITHOUT A FIGHT.

Drop down quickly and make a U-turn into the passage out of the room. As you leave, the chandelier is on your left.

Bear right and into a tunnel.

New Foe: Clockwork Automaton

CLOCKWORK AUTOMATON

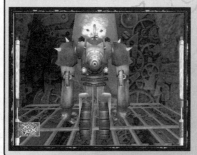

THESE MECHANIZED BEASTS ARE HELL ON WHEELS. FROM CLOSE RANGE, THEY SWING SPIKED ARMS TO DEVASTATING EFFECT. TRY TO RETREAT AND YOU GET A FACE FULL OF HOT STEAM. FINALLY, IF YOU MANAGE TO GET SOME DISTANCE BETWEEN YOU, THEY FIRE THEIR FISTS IN YOUR DIRECTION.

THE ICE WAND AND JACKS ARE EFFECTIVE IN THESE BATTLES. BOB IN AND OUT TO KEEP THE CLOCKWORK AUTOMATONS STUCK BETWEEN THEIR SHORT AND MID-RANGE ATTACKS.

Go left and left again into a tunnel.

Don't go through the next tunnel straight ahead, but instead turn right and continue.

The mirror in the corner bursts, revealing a Phantasmagoria and a peek behind the scenes.

Walk to the corner ahead but don't turn right yet. Turn to face the mirror to your left. The glass breaks to reveal a Phantasmagoria. It also reveals some of the guts of this funhouse: several steam pipes and a clock on the wall.

Break the clock from here and march toward the opening you've just created.

Break the clock with a projectile weapon. Through the glass next to the clock, a wall opens. This is where you're headed.

Continue down the hall to the right. Turn left into the tunnel. Trudge straight and into a tunnel. This brings you to a T-intersection. To the left is the newly opened wall. Go right first. You'll return here in a moment.

After you've finished with the Clockwork Automaton, look around for a set of Jacks.

A Clockwork Automaton bursts through the mirror directly ahead. Inside his lair is a very powerful new Toy: the Jacks.

New Toy: Jacks

JACKS

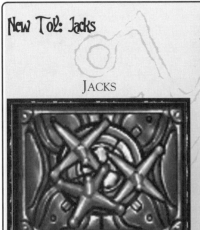

JACKS ARE ONE OF THE MOST EFFECTIVE TOYS WHEN YOU CONSIDER POWER IN RELATION TO COST. JACKS DO TREMENDOUS, AUTOMATED DAMAGE FOR A RELATIVELY SMALL AMOUNT OF STRENGTH OF WILL.

WHEN YOU THROW THE JACKS IN PRIMARY ATTACK MODE, THEY DANCE AROUND RANDOMLY, PUMMELING ANY ENEMY THEY ENCOUNTER. THEY WON'T SEEK TARGETS, BUT THEY LATCH ONTO ONE WHEN THEY FIND ONE. YOU CAN'T THROW ANOTHER HANDFUL OF JACKS UNTIL THESE RETURN TO YOU—YOU CAN, HOWEVER, SWITCH TO A DIFFERENT WEAPON AND DOUBLE YOUR ATTACK.

THE SECONDARY ATTACK IS YOUR MOST EFFECTIVE SEEKING-PROJECTILE WEAPON. THE ENTIRE SET OF JACKS DOGGEDLY PURSUES A SELECTED TARGET AND HITS IT HARD.

From the Jacks, the now-open tunnel is directly ahead.

Leave this alcove and head straight toward the open wall.

Rotating Tunnel

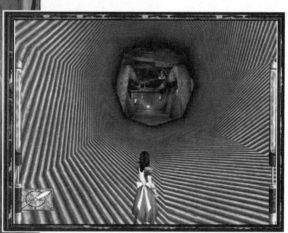

Mow down the Phantasmagoria as the tunnel rotates 90 degrees. There's a Darkened Looking Glass to collect. Turn toward the entrance of the tunnel to find it.

After the tunnel finishes its quarter-turn rotation, turn around and enter the first of two nearly identical halls.

When it stops moving, there are hallways at each end of the tunnel. Turn back the way you came and cover the left hallway first.

Left Asylum Hall

Look carefully along the walls and ceiling beams for several Nightmare Spiders.

New Foe: Nightmare Spiders

NIGHTMARE SPIDERS

YOU MAY NOT EVEN NOTICE THESE NIGHTMARE SPIDERS HANGING FROM THE CEILING. THEIR BITE IS PAINFUL AND CAUSES A TEMPORARY, MINOR BLINDNESS. FROM LONG DISTANCES, THEY SPIT GREEN VENOM.

DON'T FEEL TOO CONFIDENT IF YOU GET SOME DISTANCE BETWEEN YOU AND A NIGHTMARE SPIDER. THEY CAN SPRAY A WEB TO THE CEILING AND SWING RIGHT IN FRONT OF YOU IN THE BLINK OF AN EYE.

THE ICE WAND PROVIDES VALUABLE IMMOBILIZATION OF THESE SPEEDY THREATS.

Smash the clocks in all of the accessible rooms.

Enter each of the unlocked doors in this hallway. Dark rooms can't be opened.

Break the clock in each room with a projectile attack. There are four in this hall.

Don't go through the door at the end of this hall; it's a very costly waste of time at this point.

Return to the rotating tunnel and pass through to the other hallway.

Right Asylum Hall

Repeat the clock-breaking process in this hall. One clock is already broken (as you saw in the opening cinematic), leaving only three. When you break the last clock, a door somewhere in the complex bursts open.

When you're finished, go through the door at the end of the hall, but watch your step.

Go through two doors at the end of the hall.

Tilting Room

Navigate this area to get to the door on the upper level's opposite side. The various floors tilt in dangerous directions. For each tilting floor section, figure out how to make it balance by standing in the center or moving from one end to the other. It's important to stay on the platforms; a fall is fatal.

The Boojums are a profound danger in this constantly shifting area. Battle them on solid ground.

Tip

JUMP OUT ONTO THE FIRST TILTING PLATFORM TO ATTRACT THE ATTENTION OF THE BOOJUMS AND THEN JUMP BACK INTO THE DOORWAY. THIS ALLOWS YOU TO FIGHT FROM SOLID GROUND.

Move forward, pausing to kill off the scads of Boojums. Choose a balanced area from which to fight and stay away from the edges of the floor.

Spiral to the upper level via this path to the right. Careful—it's not as solid as it looks.

Go right at the far end of the room and follow the walkway to the upper level.

Stand in the center of the platform to balance its side-to-side tilt. Face the high room ahead (not the one filled with Insane Children).

Tilt the floor up to make the jump to the high room.

Move back to tilt the platform up toward the high room. Run and jump to it as the platform drops under your weight.

Turn around and leap toward the Roman numeral "X" floating above the room.

Follow the Roman numerals to find the Rage Box.

Leap to the next numeral (III) and to the next (IV). Bound to the roof of the room below to nab a Rage Box.

Race to the doorway.

Immediately, jump back down to the platform and jump to the large wooden double doors.

Disintegrate the Phantasmagoria and enter the large boiler room.

Boiler Room

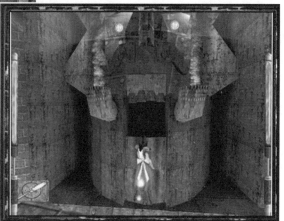

The boilers open their gaping mouths when you move in front of them. Jump and dodge to keep from being sucked into the toxic mercury sludge below.

The large boilers have eerie faces built into them. When they open their mouths, anything in front of them is sucked into a vortex. As an added hazard, the water below is rife with toxic mercury sludge— substantial damage awaits unwilling swimmers.

Note

IF YOU'RE KNOCKED INTO THE WATER, IMMEDIATELY GET TO DRY LAND AND CLIMB UP THE ROPES.

Exterminate all of the Boojums and Clockwork Automatons among the boilers.

Eliminate the Clockwork Automaton in the distance; you don't want him lobbing grenades while you're on this narrow walkway.

Turn left down the walkway. Disable the distant Clockwork Automaton from the greatest possible range. Jump through the three swinging tubes to reach the other side.

Carefully time your jumps between these tubes.

Stroll down the walkway to the door.

Tweedledee and Tweedledum

These dullards may not be too bright, but they're tough as all get-out. The hard part, however, is knowing which one to attack. The pair attack in several ways.

These guys really move when they charge with their swords.

Redefining the term "propellerhead," the Tweedles can fly and flop right on your head. You don't want that.

When they split open, expect another little Tweedle to enter the fray.

♣ The brutes pull swords out of their throats and beat you with them.

♣ The Tweedles sprout propellers from their heads, hover above you, and plummet to the ground in either a mighty stomp or a belly flop.

♣ If you get too far away, you will see a steady flow of grenades.

♣ Finally, and most annoyingly, Tweedledee and Tweedledum can split themselves open and produce lots of little Tweedles. These little clones have the same attacks as the corpulent two. Fortunately, you can maim and dispose of them quite easily.

Fighting the Tweedles involves constant motion. The Fire Jack and Jackbomb are the best attacks against the Tweedles. Given the scarcity of Meta-Essence Crystals here, you might want to rely substantially on hand-to-hand combat.

The Ice Wand is a good choice for the initial assault. Hit when the Tweedles are occupied pulling swords from their gullets.

Focus on one of the Tweedles, thereby reducing the threat by half when you kill the first one. Start with the smaller (Tweedledum). Blast him with everything you have and then cut-and-dodge with your Vorpal Blade or Mallet. Soak up his Meta-Essence and move on to the larger brother.

Use the ramp to your advantage.

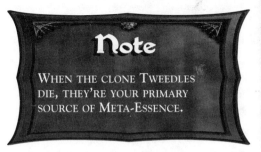

Note

WHEN THE CLONE TWEEDLES DIE, THEY'RE YOUR PRIMARY SOURCE OF META-ESSENCE.

Don't waste attacks on the clone Tweedles (though some are similar in size to their likenesses).

When the brothers are eviscerated, you receive a greeting from the Hatter and are forcibly sucked into his realm.

Chapter 9
Behind the Looking Glass

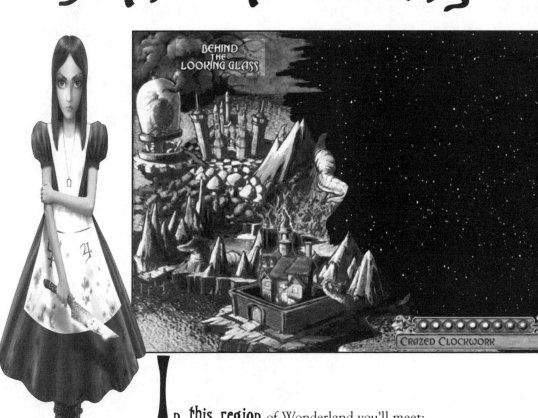

CRAZED CLOCKWORK

In **this region** of Wonderland you'll meet:

Friends

♣ March Hare
♣ Dormouse
♣ Gryphon

Foes

♣ Nightmare Spider
♣ Clockwork Automaton
♣ Boojum
♣ Phantasmagoria
♣ Mad Hatter (boss)

Crazed Clockwork

Front Porch

Start forward and rough up the Boojum. Jump over to the Hatter's front porch and burst through the front door.

Head toward the porch on the right. You won't go to the Clock Tower until later.

Note

NOTICE A PORTAL ON THE CLOCK TOWER LEFT OF THE FRONT DOOR. RETURN TO THAT AREA LATER.

Foyer

Walk under the ticking clock and follow the path to the right.

Switch Room

Walk around both sides of this room and pull the switches located on each side.

Pull the switches on both sides of the room to create a way across the pool.

After both switches have been pulled, a large cog rises from the water in the center of the room. Jump onto it and cross to a hallway.

Turn left and go through the large door.

Sinking Clocks

Climb the stairs and turn right to a room with floating clocks.

There's a pot of Grasshopper Tea under the stairs.

The mercury in this room is deadly and some of these clocks can't withstand the weight of a person standing on them. How do you know which ones will sink?

Note

BELOW THE STAIRS IS A DOSE OF GRASSHOPPER TEA. DRINKING IT MAKES NAVIGATING THE NEXT ROOM MUCH EASIER. AFTER DRINKING THE TEA, STEP TO THE LEFT CORNER OF THE PLATFORM AND YOU'LL RISE TO THE LANDING ABOVE. THEN HOP TO THE SWITCH IN THE NEXT ROOM.

The mirror to the left reveals which clocks are stable. Start with the two rows between yourself and the switch.

Look in the mirror to your left: The unsteady clocks appear faceless in the mirror. The stable clocks are simple mirror images.

As you look at the two rows of clocks in front of you, jump in this order:

1. First on right.
2. Second on left.
3. Third on right.

Pull the switch and follow this pattern:

1. First on left.
2. Second on right.
3. Third on left.

To get to the newly opened door, use these two rows of clocks.

Turn to face left and follow this pattern:

1. Second on right (skip the first row).
2. Fourth on right.

Jump to the ledge.

Upstairs Hallway

The door seals behind you.

Investigate to the right down the hallway to find a barred door. You come back up through that door after unlocking it.

Remember this spot; you come back through it after it's unlocked.

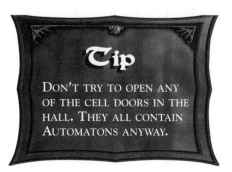

Tip

DON'T TRY TO OPEN ANY OF THE CELL DOORS IN THE HALL. THEY ALL CONTAIN AUTOMATONS ANYWAY.

Go back to where you entered the hall and go straight.

A Boojum attacks from the left. The door it guards is locked by a giant key protruding from the floor. You can't unlock it.

Return to the hall and continue, turning right at the corner.

This door is locked, too, and that key's too big to turn. Find another way to unlock it.

The double doors at the end are locked, but an open cell to your right has a hole in its floor. Be ready to fight as you drop down the hole.

Drop through the hole in the floor.

Follow the hall to large double doors. Enter the lab.

Lab Foyer

Stomp on the two Nightmare Spiders and head through the open hallway opposite the stairs.

The hall opposite the stairs leads to the lab.

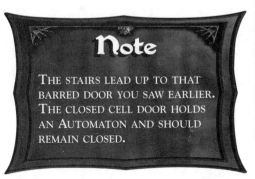

Note

THE STAIRS LEAD UP TO THAT BARRED DOOR YOU SAW EARLIER. THE CLOSED CELL DOOR HOLDS AN AUTOMATON AND SHOULD REMAIN CLOSED.

The Lab

You find the very unfortunate March Hare and Dormouse. You also witness the gruesome process by which the Hatter is building his Automaton minions.

Pull the switch to open the barred doors. The Hatter unlocks the room near the giant key.

After an unsettling exchange with the
Dormouse and March Hare, pull this switch to
unlock the barred door and, indirectly, the
doors near the giant key.

The barred doors atop these
stairs are now open.

Return to the Lab Foyer and take
the stairs up to the upstairs hallway.

Thanks to the Hatter,
you can pass through here.

Upstairs Hallway

Turn right and go to the now-unlocked door.

Room of Stairs

Slaughter the Nightmare Spider and follow the steps to the left.

Destroy the Phantasmagoria, who is guarding another set double doors. Go inside and talk with the Gryphon. The final Demon Die is beside the Gryphon, and there's a Super Meta-Essence crystal on the other side of the staircase.

Go through this door to get a more levelheaded description of what's going on in this horrible place.

Turn and head back out the door. Follow the stairs to the right and gut the Nightmare Spiders waiting for you.

Venture through two doors and find yourself back in the Foyer.

Work your way over to this platform.

Foyer, Again

Cross the bridge and give the Nightmare Spider a swift kick.
Go through the door and climb up to the portal you saw from the Front Porch.

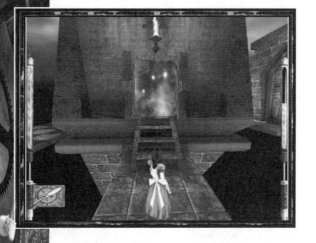

Vault into the portal to attend the Mad Hatter's new tea-party.

Tea Table

The portal takes you to a gigantic table set for tea.

Jump onto each of the four sugar cubes in the cups of tea. When all four have submerged, the clock at the end of the table descends and reveals a portal.

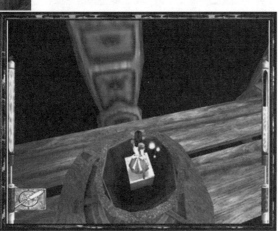

Step very briefly on each sugar lump. Don't get burned!

Tip

THE TEA IS VERY HOT, SO JUMP OUT OF THE CUP QUICKLY.

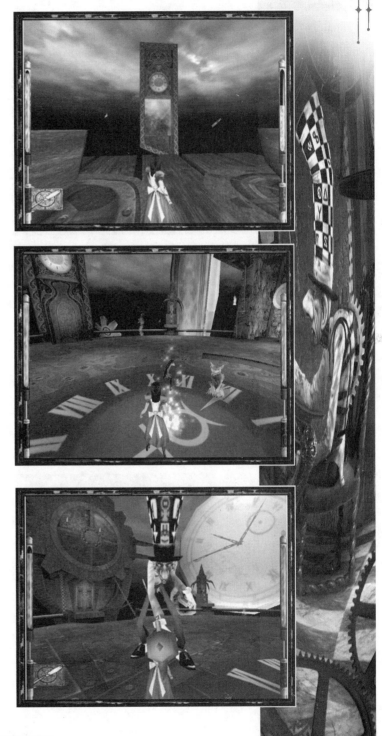

After all four cubes have been dunked, the clock opens.

Leap into the portal.

Clock Tower

Walk straight into the belly of the Clock Tower. Pull the switch.

About Face

The second piece of the coveted Eyestaff is in the ceter of the Hatter's arena.

Enter the Hatter's arena and go to the center. Before the mayhem begins, lay claim to the second piece of the Jabberwock's Eyestaff. After you have it, the Hatter appears on the scene.

At last you get your shot at the Mad Hatter. Unfortunately, you're on his turf in this time-obsessed arena. Beware his awesome powers.

The Hatter is murder with that cane.

Anyone for tea? Not when it comes out of someone's hat.

Spider syringes cause disorientation and partial blindness. Very dangerous on this precarious platform.

When the Hatter disappears, be ready to fight a pair of Clockwork Automatons.

♣ At close range, the Hatter swings at you with either his cane or his hand. If you're at medium distance, he sprints forward and swings with one or the other for increased damage.

♣ Teacup bombs launch from his hat and careen around the arena.

♣ Missiles fire from his fingertips. These weapons are tipped with Nightmare Spider venom, producing the same disorientation effect.

♣ Frequently, the Hatter disappears and is replaced by two Clockwork Automatons. After they're vanquished, the Hatter returns.

Your only source for Meta-Essence in this fight is defeated Automatons. The Hatter has one weakness: Jacks. He can't stand the chaos they create. Immediately circle strafe the Hatter at medium distance: It's too far for him to hit you with his fist or cane and too close for other attacks. Launch a Jack attack at every opportunity. If you play it right, the Hatter doesn't stand a chance.

Circle strafe the Hatter relentlessly and pummel him with Jacks.

Your reward? A tremendous cranial explosion!

Warning
WHEN CIRCLE STRAFING, DON'T FALL OFF THE PLATFORM.

After the Hatter's head has detonated, the clock adjacent to the arena begins to run.

Ride the weights to get into the clock's inner works.

Jump on the weights when they drop to ground level and ride them up into the works of the clock.

Nab the Dead Time Watch. The walkway around the clock contains a large Meta-Essence.

Here is a nifty time-stopping power-up to boot.

After both prizes are yours, you'll pay a visit to the Gryphon.

Chapter 10
Land of Fire and Brimstone

BURNING CURIOSITY

In this region of Wonderland you'll meet:

Friends

♣ Gryphon

Foes

♣ Fire Imp

♣ Fire Snark

♣ Jabberspawn

♣ Boojum

♣ Jabberwock (Boss)

♣ Spade Card Guard

♣ Heart Card Guard

To boost your budding arsenal of deadly Toys, you'll find:

♣ Jabberwock Eyestaff
♣ Blunderbuss

Burning Curiosity

Canyon

You'll need to walk for awhile to get through this lava-encrusted valley.

Push straight ahead into this gigantic canyon full of Fire Imps.

The power-ups in this lava pool are more trouble than they're worth thanks to the Fire Snark.

At the far end, a large lava pool bubbles to the left. If you require a boost in Strength of Will, jump over the rocks in this pool, but keep two things in mind. First, some of the rocks (including the one that holds the Vials of Will) may sink if you stand on them. Second, the pool is home to a Fire Snark. It's not worth the risk.

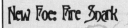

New Foe: Fire Snark

FIRE SNARK

THE FIRE SNARK IS SIMILAR TO ITS WATER-DWELLING COUSIN, BUT MORE DANGEROUS. WATCH LAVA POOLS FOR SMALL RIPPLES AND CLOUDS OF STEAM THAT INDICATE THE PRESENCE OF ONE OF THESE FISH BENEATH THE SURFACE.

FIRE SNARKS LEAP FROM THE WATER AND SPIT FIREBALLS. BUT WHAT MAKES THEM TRULY DANGEROUS IS THE FAMILIAR TONGUE ATTACK. BEING PULLED INTO A DARK LAKE BY A SNARK TONGUE IS SCARY, BUT THE SAME FATE IN A LAVA POOL IS FATAL. THEY ALSO BITE, BUT YOU'LL BURN TO DEATH BEFORE YOU DISCOVER THIS.

At the end of the canyon, find the start of the path up the wall.

Move toward the right side of the canyon and climb the canyon wall. Navigable ledges line the wall as you travel from bottom to top, right to left.

About halfway up, jump up onto a high rock to continue.

The Canyon Wall

At the top of the wall, peer up the path to see a pair of Jabberspawns.

THE JABBERSPAWNS ARE SMALLER, LAND-BOUND VERSIONS OF THEIR LEGENDARY MASTER. WITH A LIGHTNING ATTACK, A FEROCIOUS CLAW SWIPE, AND A KNEECAP-BUSTING TAIL WHIP, THE JABBERSPAWN IS A DANGEROUS BEAST. JACKS WORK SPECTACULARLY WELL AGAINST THEM.

Spelunk into the first cave.

Fire Cave, Part 1

You're greeted by a Boojum. Leap over the lava pool to the left.

Warning

THE LAVA POOLS HERE ARE INHABITED BY FIRE SNARKS.

You've interrupted these Fire Imps' shower in the lava fall. Time to ruin their day even more.

Two Fire Imps leap from a lava fall. Uphill, two Jabberspawns pace like caged dogs.

Climb the green rock to mount this ledge.

At a high wall, jump onto a green rock to scale the ledge. Instantly, a Magma Man surfaces in the lava pool to the left.

*Use these rocks
to cross the lava stream.*

Hop on the rocks to the opposite side of the lava stream. Move quickly—some rocks may sink if you stand on them.

You end up back on the right shore. Pull yourself up the rocks to look at daylight again.

Fire Ravine

Go to the left.

Hop toward the left shore of the stream. Cross the river several times by jumping on the rocks.

Fight the Jabberspawn long distance using alternate attacks with cards or the Croquet Mallet. Then jump to his perch.

*Move into this second cave.
Don't forget the Rage
Box across the stream.*

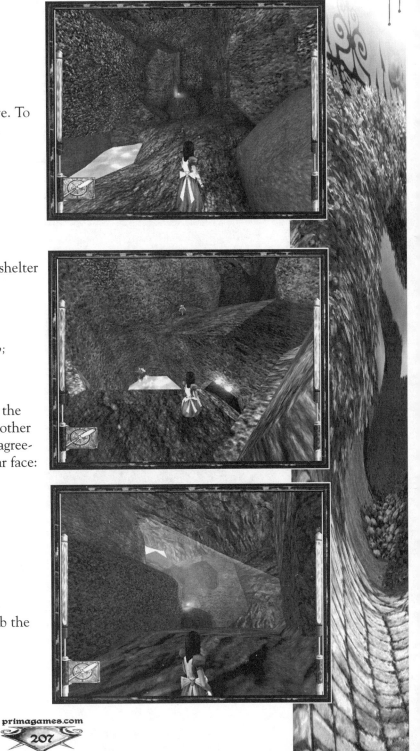

The path turns into another cave. To
the left is another Rage Box. Use it.

Fire Cave, Part 2

Freeze the Boojum as you enter the shelter
of the cave.

*Fire Snarks complicate your jump;
they await you in this gap.*

Jump over a gap and extinguish the
Fire Imps. Move forward to have another
encounter with the Oracle. The disagree-
able Oracle turns out to be a familiar face:
Caterpillar.

*This stream of daylight marks
the way out of the cave.*

Walk toward the light and climb the
high wall.

Pull yourself up this steep wall to reach the great outdoors.

Alice's House

Home sweet home.

Back in daylight, the convergence of Alice's damaged psyche and the state of Wonderland are revealed. High on a hill, Alice confronts her own home, untouched by fire.

Drop down to follow the dangerous path to the house.

Hopscotch along the rocks to the right. A Magma Man emerges from the fire, but don't waste time standing to fight.

This climb is brutal and very precarious. Jump and climb carefully.

Pull yourself up on several small ledges and make many precarious jumps. After you reach the house, mow down the Jabberspawn and Fire Imp.

This portal takes you to the Jabberwock's Lair.

Head through the portal in the house's front door.

Jabberwock's Lair

This is the first of two encounters with the mighty Jabberwock. This Jabberwock, however, has more than jaws that bite and claws that catch.

The eye lasers are most powerful.

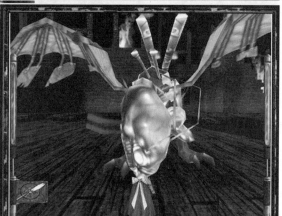

Chomp! So, his bite is worse than his bark.

Twin Jabberspawns periodically join the party. Kill them to gain Meta-Essence.

♣ Of course, it does have those claws that bite and they're nasty.

♣ It fires an energy beam from its eyes. The beam follows you if you move while this attack is under way.

♣ Periodically, pairs of Jabberspawns leap into the fray. Killing them is your only source of Meta-Essence.

♣ The Jabberwock's fire breath is easy to avoid but does severe and ongoing damage when it strikes.

The fire breath keeps you burning for several seconds after the attack.

The normally flying Jabberwock stays grounded in this battle. He occasionally leaps to attack, but his wings never come into play.

As with the Hatter, the auto-targeting Jacks are your best choice of Toys. Unlike with the Hatter, however, the stunt is much harder to pull off. Circle strafe to attack.

Circle strafing with Jacks is a successful strategy.

When the Jabberspawns appear, disengage from the Jabberwock and attack the smaller monsters with either Jacks or the Ice Wand. Scoop up their Meta-Essence and return to the Jabberwock.

If you can fend off the Jabberwock for a short time, Gryphon will swoop in and tear out the Jabberwock's eye—this is the last piece of the Eyestaff. The severely injured Jabberwock flees.

New Toy: Jabberwock Eyestaff

JABBERWOCK EYESTAFF

THE EYESTAFF IS A STUNNINGLY POWERFUL TOY BUT HAS SEVERAL STRATEGIC DISADVANTAGES.

IN PRIMARY FIRE MODE, HOLD THE ATTACK BUTTON WHILE THE EYESTAFF CHARGES. YOU MAY MOVE DURING THIS PERIOD. AFTER THE STAFF IS CHARGED, IT EMITS THE JABBERWOCK'S PURPLE ENERGY BEAM. WHEN YOU RELEASE THE ATTACK BUTTON, THE BEAM ENDS IN A POWERFUL EXPLOSION. THE BEAM PERSISTS AS LONG AS YOU HOLD THE ATTACK BUTTON AND CONSUMES CONSIDERABLE STRENGTH OF WILL.

ALTERNATE FIRE MODE IS A WHOLE DIFFERENT AFFAIR. YOU MUST STAND STILL DURING A CONSIDERABLE CHARGING PERIOD. THE LONGER YOU HOLD THE BUTTON, THE MORE POWERFUL THE WEAPON'S SHOT WILL BE. WHEN THE WEAPON IS FULLY CHARGED OR YOU RELEASE THE BUTTON, SEVERAL FLARES ROCKET SKYWARD AND SOON PLUMMET BACK TO EARTH IN SHATTERING EXPLOSIONS.

The last piece of the Jabberwock Eyestaff is yours.

Grab the eye.

Caterpillar's Plot, Revisited

Canyon of Fire

You are standing in front of the Jabberwock's Lair. Straight ahead and down this hill is the pass to the Majestic Maze and Queen of Hearts Land—this is where you're ultimately bound.

Pay a visit to Humpty Dumpty. He doesn't talk much—too busy picking his own brain—but he does reveal a secret. Jump onto the ledge to the right of him and press the protruding brick into the wall.

*Stand next to Humpty to
open a secret area.*

*The wall opens to expose
a hidden hallway.*

Next, head into the tunnel you took earlier to visit the Oracle. It's blocked off, but a secret door is now open on the left.

The Blunderbuss is your prize.

Venture into the hall to snag the Blunderbuss, the last Toy.

New Toy: Blunderbuss

BLUNDERBUSS

THE BLUNDERBUSS IS THE WORLD'S MOST POWERFUL MUSKET. THE IMPOSSIBLY HUGE SHOT IT FIRES BURSTS FROM THE GUN'S BELL, KNOCKING ALICE BACKWARD, AND DETONATES AT ITS TARGET.

THE ENSUING EXPLOSION SEVERELY DAMAGES EVERYTHING NEAR THE POINT OF IMPACT.

PRIMARY AND ALTERNATE ATTACK ARE THE SAME, BUT BOTH DEVOUR YOUR ENTIRE SUPPLY OF STRENGTH OF WILL. YOU CAN'T USE THIS TOY IF YOU HAVE LESS THAN FULL STRENGTH OF WILL.

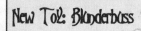

The signposts point the way.

Follow the signposts to the "Majestic Maze." As you enter the pass, beat up a Fire Imp.

The valley of Cards is a dangerous place.

Farther along, outsmart and out duel an array of Card Guards, including several Spade and Heart Card Guards.

New Foe: Spade Card Guards

SPADE CARD GUARDS

THE SPADE CARD GUARDS POSSESS BOTH KILLER MELEE MOVES AND A NASTY PROJECTILE ATTACK.
WHEN IN ARM'S REACH, SPADE CARD GUARDS HAVE SEVERAL DIFFERENT, VERY FAST SWINGS WITH THEIR SPEARS. FROM FARTHER AWAY THEY CAN FIRE GRENADES FROM THE ENDS OF THE SAME WEAPON—THEY HURT YOU AND THROW YOU BACK SEVERAL FEET.

New Foe: Heart Card Guard

HEART CARD GUARD

THE QUEEN'S ELITE GUARDS ARE THE TOUGHEST OF ALL. THEIR MELEE MOVES ARE THE SNAZZIEST AND QUICKEST OF ALL. FIGHTING THEM HAND TO HAND IS A REAL CHALLENGE.
FROM A DISTANCE, THEY HAVE A HIGHLY EXPLOSIVE PROJECTILE ATTACK. IT'S VERY DIFFICULT TO DODGE BUT TAKES SOME TIME TO CHARGE. IF YOU CAN CATCH THEM DURING THE CHARGING INTERVAL, YOU CAN DEAL OUT AN UNANSWERABLE ATTACK.

At the far end of this canyon, approach the barrier prohibiting your entrance into Queen of Hearts Land.

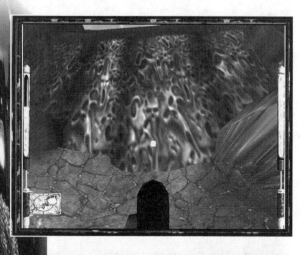

This barrier prevents you entering the Queen's domain.

Fire the Jabberwock Eyestaff to punch a hole.

Fire the Jabberwock's Eyestaff at the wall to blast a hole. Pass though.

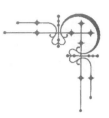

Chapter 11
Queen of Hearts Land

QUEEN OF HEARTS LAND

MAJESTIC MAZE

In this region of Wonderland you'll meet:

Foes

♣ Boojum

♣ Spade Card Guard

♣ Heart Card Guard

♣ Phantasmagoria

♣ Jabberspawn

♣ Snark

♣ Clockwork Automaton

Majestic Maze

Start—Right, Left, Left, Left

Enter the maze. Turn left at the corner and head uphill. An array of Card Guards greets you.

Beware the Jabberspawns, my Alice.

As you near the next corner, two Jabberspawns spring from above: one ahead and one behind. Follow the trail to the left. Mow down the Card Guards and take the first left.

Ambush—Second Right, Right

The trail looks clear until you take the second right. Suddenly the Heart Guards are all over you.

Take the second right, but backpedal when the gang of Heart Card Guards jumps into action. As you retreat, be aware of a Jabberspawn that's popped up behind you. After everyone's vanquished, go around the corner to the right.

The Rage Box and the Portal—Right, Second Left

The Rage Box helps you get through the thick pack of baddies ahead.

As you approach the T-intersection ahead, pick up the Rage Box and dive into the opposition: a Phantasmagoria, a Jabberspawn, and a Boojum.

You can't go into this portal because it's an exit. The other side of it is in the maze's final room.

Go right at the T-intersection. As you go downhill, you pass the arrival side of a portal on your right.

Note

A PORTAL IN THIS MAZE'S FINAL ROOM LEADS BACK TO THIS EXIT PORTAL.

As you approach the next corner, you face several Card Guards and a Phantasmagoria from the front and a Boojum from the rear.

Corner left and spin around to fight the Jabberspawn that's pounced behind you.

After the coast is clear, duck through this doorway.

Heart-Shaped Doors and Exit

Pass through the heart-shaped doorway. Emerging on the other side of the hedge, do battle with several Boojums and Diamond and Club Card Guards. Leave all but one Club Card Guard alive.

The exit portal is through that massive door. Bring some Card Guards with you if you deign to let any live.

Pass through the larger heart-shaped doorway. Walk on either side of the divider. When the paths rejoin, go through the next heart-shaped doorway.

The exit portal is blocked by an iron gate. The pressure plate on the left opens the gate. The portal on the right leads back into the maze.

As you enter, an Insane Child steps on a pressure plate to the left. This opens the gate to the level exit but only so long as someone's standing on it. The Insane Child then dives into the other portal (taking him to the exit portal we saw earlier).

Bring a foe with you to stand on that plate so you can pass through the gate and the exit.

Retrace your steps to find the reinforcements that have reclaimed the maze.

Lead a Card Guard back to the pressure plate and let him act as weight. Run into the exit portal.

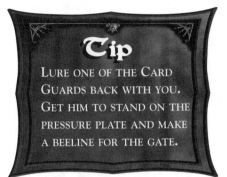

After you're safely on the other side of the gate, step through the portal.

Airborne Terror

Part 1

From here you can see the exit, but you can't get to it.

If you look up from your starting point, you can see the portal to which you're headed. Getting there will require some daring and lots of steam.

Ride the steam to the platform straight ahead and left of your starting position.

Warning

HERE YOU'LL BE AMBUSHED BY A BOOJUM. THEY'LL AMBUSH YOU THROUGHOUT THIS CLIMB. YOU KNOW HOW TO HANDLE SUCH DIFFICULTIES AND WHAT THE DANGERS ARE. BE READY FOR ATTACKS AT ANY MOMENT.

Let this vent carry you to the next platform.

Turn right and ride the vent to a lower platform. When you land, climb up a small bridge and follow the walkway around to the left as it winds up the column. At the top, turn right and follow the long series of steam vents.

Take your time to navigate these stacks without incident.

Tip

ADJUST YOUR VIEW SO YOU'RE LOOKING DOWN ON ALICE. AS YOU MOVE TO EACH VENT, STABILIZE YOURSELF OVER THE VENT BEFORE MOVING TO THE NEXT ONE OR ELSE YOU'LL CAREEN OUT OF CONTROL.

These masks spew steam that will knock you out of the range of the stacks that are keeping you aloft. Don't pass them until they stop blowing.

After the first couple of vents, look for masks on the wall that spew horizontal steam jets. These will instantly knock you out of the air and into the lava below. Pause on the vent before each mask, wait for it to stop firing, then move to the next stack.

After you arrive at the wooden platform, turn right and climb the walkway.

At the top, turn right and use the single vent to float to the next platform.

Move through this doorway.

Part Two

Climb the ramp and enter the doorway.

Follow the passage until you reach another platform below the exit portal.

Turn left and climb the walkway. After several Boojums, you arrive at the top platform.

This string of stacks is even more difficult.

To continue, ride another very long string of vents. There's a mask near the second to last.

There's only one vent mask to worry about.

Land safely on the platform and turn left to follow the walkway to its end.

High, higher, highest.

Ride up a series of three increasingly tall vent stacks. Drop onto the wooden platform and turn left.

This door leads to the exit portal. No more floating for a while.

Follow the walkway through a door and pop into the portal.

Mystifying Madness

Start up either of the staircases and into the maze. Follow the path to a T-intersection, where you'll be ambushed by a Spade Card Guard, a Jabberspawn, and (behind you) a Phantasmagoria.

Before you can go through that door, some folks want to have a word with you.

Turn right and follow the path. As it nears a doorway, a similar ambush awaits.

Enter the doorway and turn right at the first courtyard to find a diamond-shaped hole in the ground.

This hole leads to the underground lake.

As you approach, two Jabberspawns and a Phantasmagoria jump into view.

Prepare for some serious swimming, and dive into the hole. To help you get your bearings when you arrive at the floor of the lake, face the pool as shown in the image here (looking at the path from which the Phantasmagoria came).

To be properly oriented when you reach the bottom of the lake, face this direction before diving in.

Dive to the bottom and immediately filet the two Snarks.

Use the Meta-Essence Crystal as a landmark before consuming it.

Swim straight (toward the small Meta-Essence Crystal) into a tunnel.

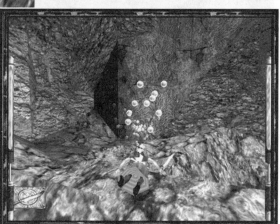

The bubbles provide a timely refueling for your air supply.

As you emerge from the tunnel, refill your Mock Turtle Shell at the bubble flow.

This lamp is the next landmark. Swim toward it.

Turn right and swim toward the diamond-shaped light. As you pass under the light, submerge straight down to fight a Snark and refresh at another bubble flow.

Swim around to the right. Knife a couple of Snarks and surface to look for a shore with a long string of Meta-Essence Crystals.

Look for this string of Meta-Essence Crystals to find a way out of the lake.

Hop up onto shore. Vaporize the Spade Card Guard across the room and take the very long leap to the closest solid ground (it looks too far but it's not).

Look for the metal walkway. It's best to fight all those Card Guards from here.

Follow the ledge around to a stone platform and turn right to find a metal walkway.

Lob a couple of Jackbombs down the hall to wipe out the Spade and Heart Card Guard squad.

The switch allows you to get back up to the surface and, eventually, the exit.

Continue straight to find a switch. Pull it. This opens an underwater gate directly below your current position.

Turn around quickly to fight two Clockwork Automatons who've appeared on the scene.

Go through this door.

Go right. Descend the stairs and follow the hall to a metal spiral staircase guarded by two Heart Card Guards. Climb the stairs and stroll along the catwalk to a T-intersection.

Go right and jump atop a short wall.

Cross the pipe.

Carefully, cross the pipe and jump through the doorway. Stroll down the passage until you come to a doorway filled by a large Meta-Essence Crystal.

Look for this opening to return to the underground lake.

Drop into the water and submerge to the bottom. Swim toward the diamond-shaped light. This brings you to the large pool. Follow the wall to the left.

Seek out this tunnel but get a good shell full of air first.

Swim into a tunnel marked by a clover-shaped light. As you swim, stop at both of the bubble flows to refill your supply. Slaughter the two Snarks and swim to the large bubble flow over the metal grate.

This is the gate you lowered with the switch. Swim in and to the surface.

Swim straight to the surface. Back on dry land, shoot the Heart Card Guard down the path.

Follow the path to a T-intersection. Go left and take the first right after beating down the Boojum and Card Guards.

Cross the bridge.

Turn left to cross the bridge, then go right. Follow the garden path to the left. Turn left. Rub out the Card Guards and turn right to find a switch.

From this alcove, you can see the exit. To get to it, pull the switch here.

From here you can see the exit portal in a courtyard below, but it's behind an iron gate. Pull the switch here and the iron gate opens to clear the way.

Turn around and go to the right to where the path ends at a ledge. Turn to face the way you came.

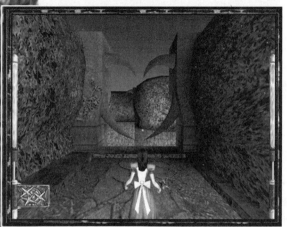

Approach the ledge at the end of the path, turn around, and drop down backward to be ready to fight when your feet touch the ground.

Back off the path and drop to the lower path. Deactivate the Automaton, and go straight and left to the portal courtyard.

Clear out the opposition and walk confidently into the exit portal.

Obliterate the two Heart Card Guards and freely enter the waiting portal.

Water Logged

Water Rise 1

Start with the pool in the next room.

Turn right and go through the doorway.

Turn left. Dive into the water and swim straight to the far end of the chamber.

*Go into the light! Swim as far as
you can and surface.*

Swim into a short tunnel. Turn
around and surface. Climb the ledges to
the top of the wall.

*Step onto this platform to raise the water
level one notch.*

Jump onto the hanging platform—
this raises the water level in the area.
This is the first of several jumps here.

Water Rise 2

Tip
SURFACE FOR AIR.

Take this doorway back to the other pool.

Swim straight from the hanging platform and turn right to enter a doorway that's now at water level. Walk around the central pillar and you come to this area's other pool.

Dive into this tunnel.

Look left: The water has risen to open a tunnel in the floor of this pool. Dive in and drop into that tunnel.

Slip through the holes in the grates to get to the bottom of things.

Move through the holes in the grates until you reach the bottom. Follow the tube as it turns toward a T-intersection.

Turn right immediately, and take advantage of some much needed air bubbles. Return to the T-intersection and go straight.

Stay to the left as you approach the intake fan. Rise quickly to the surface. Climb out of the water and pull yourself up the wall. Cross the bridge and turn right to climb another wall.

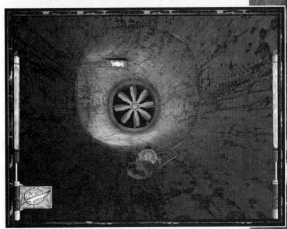

Hug the left wall to avoid being sliced.

Climb up to the second platform switch to raise the water some more.

Step onto the hanging platform to raise the water level again.

Water Rise 3

Swim forward into a newly opened tube. A bubble flow offers air replenishment.

The lid has floated on this tube. Dive into it for the next step.

Move into a T-intersection. Go right for another bubble flow. Go through the T-intersection and toward a series of intake fans.

Stay to the left; there's an intake fan on the right side of the tube.

Navigate around these fans and follow the tube to the left.

Stay high as you pass another intake fan in the floor of the tube. Hold to the left side as you approach the third fan. Turn left. Refill your shell on the bubble flow.

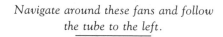

Time your ascent to squeeze through the gap in the fan.

Rise through the tunnel, looking upward. Ascend through the gaps in the fan.

Scale this tower to the next switch platform.

Climb out of the water and scale the tower to another hanging platform. Step onto it to raise the water level again.

Water Rise 4

Swim straight into a doorway and walk down the hall. Drop into the hole in the floor and swim forward into the other pool.

The last tube leads to the exit portal.

Dive into the now-open tube. Descend to the portal.

Labyrinthine Revenge

The Lava Stream

Turn left and move to the edge of this high tower.

Jump down to the small light fixture.

Look down for a light fixture lower than those surrounding the tower and drop to it. Turn right and jump down to another fixture and onto a ridge along the wall.

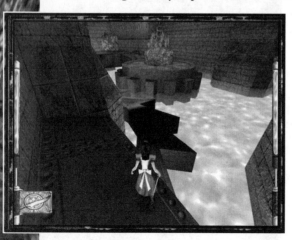

Leaping over lava is hot work but it's the only way to go.

Hop onto the spinning gear and onto the island in the middle of the lava pool. Leap to the next island and quickly (the island's sinking) jump to the next gear.

Climb to the path above.

Move around the gear. Jump onto the first light fixture and up to the path above. Run along the path until you spot a doorway across the lava stream. Drop to a light fixture and spring across to the doorway.

Wheels and Gears

Follow the hallway and up the ramp around a spinning turbine.

Use this wheel to get across.

At the top of the ramp, jump to the turbine and across to a doorway. Follow the hallway through a door.

You will fit through that hole, but time it right.

Pause by the wheel and wait for a gap to appear. Jump through it. Fight off the Clockwork Automaton and wait for a gap in the next wheel. Go through the door, turn right, and go up the ramp. Turn right and navigate the hall into the Steam Pool Room.

Steam Pool Room

A large lava pool belches steam into the air. Two Clockwork Automatons leave their duties at the control panels and turn to greet you.

This cabinet is the first step to a well-hidden Meta-Essence Crystal.

To the right of the control panel, turn right and climb atop a cabinet on the wall. Jump on the rope and climb up to a large Meta-Essence Crystal.

Trudge through the doorway left of the control panel and scale the ramp. Vaporize two Fire Imps and turn to climb the next ramp. Go left through a door.

Whirlpool Room

Turn right past a raging water pool. Turn left and wipe out a Jabberspawn. Follow the walkway to the other side of the pool and turn right through a door.

Garden Maze

Walk forward along the path. As you turn left, face down a couple of Jabberspawns.

Continue on the path as it ramps down and around.

Follow the lengthy path through the garden as it twists around. The numerous Heart and Spade Card Guards will try to stop your progress.

Continue on the path and down a series of ramps. Go through a doorway into a red-brick tunnel.

Between the Teeth

Follow the tunnel, turn right and go through the doorway. To traverse this walkway, you need to stand between the teeth of the spinning gears as they slowly spin forward.

The scald you'll get from these steam jets is nothing compared to the lava burns you'll get next.

Complicating this is a pair of bellows that blow air across the walkway. Wait for each to stop blowing before you move past it.

Step slowly forward as the gear spins, pause for the second steam jet, and venture through the door.

Follow the hallway through a door. Down the hall, short circuit the Clockwork Automaton and turn right.

Slow Gear Room

Step forward onto a large, slowly spinning gear and pause to ground two Boojums.

*This jet is your elevator
to the next floor.*

Go out onto one of the teeth and wait to come around to a vertical steam jet. Ride it up to a second jet and leap to the walkway. Destroy two Jabberspawns.

At the walkway's end, ride two steam jets up to another gear. Move forward after battling the Boojums and leap to a doorway above the wheel. Cut down a Boojum and a Clockwork Automaton as you head down a hall through a door. Turn left, then right through a door.

The Gear and the Wall

*Stand on the teeth or you'll
be knocked into the abyss.*

Jump to a spinning gear and immediately move out onto one of the teeth. When the wheel takes you around the wall, open fire on the Spade Card Guard. Rush through two doors and out into another garden maze.

Garden Maze, Part 2

Follow the pathway. Spade and Diamond Card Guards are your only opposition on the way to a courtyard graced by a small fountain.

After the Cheshire Cat fountain, master the timing of the falling tunnel barriers.

    The path out of here is blocked by a pair of rising-and-falling barriers. Wait for the first to rise and step past it. Do the same with the second.

    Turn right and gut a Spade Card Guard, and take out a Heart Card Guard in the distance.

    This passage is blocked by two swinging barriers. Again, wait for each to pass before proceeding.

The timing here is a bit tougher. Rid yourself of the Card Guard before doing anything.

    Scale the ramp and head through a door. Continue up the ramp and back up to the garden.

Ride the pipes up to the high ledge.

Use the vertical steam pipes to arrive at a high ledge. Turn right and slip through a door.

Gear Catwalk

Walk between the teeth of three gigantic gears as they rotate before you.

You don't have much time to pass under these large gears.

Follow the hallway to a courtyard and pop through the portal.

Machinations

Clockwork Room 1

I hope you're not under the influence of anything that would make you fear heavy machinery. No? Good. Walk toward the thick rotating gear on your level.

Climb the gear stairs.

Look for a series of three horizontal gears, each higher than the one before. Jump to the lowest and up to the third.

Tip

YOU CAN ADJUST THE LANDING PLACE OF YOUR JUMPS WHILE IN THE AIR. IF YOU'VE MISJUDGED SLIGHTLY, YOU CAN MAKE ADJUSTMENTS WHILE AIRBORNE.

Leap to the solid checkerboard floor. Jump to the barrel-shaped gear when it lowers into jumping range. Proceed higher in the room by riding two more similar gears.

Jump between the barrel gears.

Jump from the third gear to a screw with two barrel gears; jump between them. Leap to the safety of the ledge. Follow the hallway.

Clockwork Room 2

Jump to the pedals rotating just below this ledge.

Fly to either of the pedals before you.

Leap to the next set of pedals, then to the checkerboard ledge. From there, jump to a single pedal swinging back and forth and from there to another ledge.

Collect yourself on the ledge and jump yet another set of pedals. Take the long leap to the barrel gear nearby.

When the time is right, jump into the cage-like gear.

Wait for the cage-like gear to come into range and jump inside. Switch to the nearby pedals and back onto the "roof" of the cage gear. Continue straight and over to a barrel gear when it lowers into range.

Get onto one of the teeth and ride over the top of this gear. Be ready to jump off, though.

The next gear is vertically oriented and rotating from bottom to top. Jump onto one of the teeth and ride it to the top.

Get to the checkerboard ledge before you're dumped off the gear. Go through the hall.

Clockwork Room 3

Wait for the barrel gear to rise into range before you and move to it.

As soon as you land on this gear, stand on the stationary arm and walk its length.

Look down to see a gear attached to a long arm moving back and forth across the room. Jump to it and quickly get on the arm.

Traverse the arm and jump to the small ledge on the wall. Next, head to the barrel gear to the right. When the barrel gear reaches its highest point, go to the seesaw and stand in the center to balance it.

Jump to the next thick gear straight ahead. Spin around and jump onto another seesaw.

Stand toward the far end of the seesaw to tilt it upward and gain a little extra height on your jump.

Tilt it slightly upward and jump to the next barrel gear. Look down and leap to the gigantic, horizontal, jagged-toothed wheel in the center of the room. Land around the edge or you'll fall through the spokes.

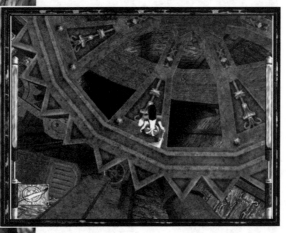

Don't fall through the spokes.

Move to the next barrel gear as it rises into jumping range. Watch the *vertical* jagged-toothed wheel and jump onto one of its teeth.

Stand in the middle of the tooth and turn right so you're looking at the lever that drops into place each time the wheel turns.

Climb up the lever to reach the exit portal.

Stand between the two arms of the lever and jump so you're standing on top of the lever.

Scale the lever to the wall and jump down to safety and the portal.

Chapter 12

Queensland

In this region of Wonderland you'll meet:

Foes:

- ♣ Jabberwock (Boss)
- ♣ Diamond Card Guard
- ♣ Spade Card Guard
- ♣ Heart Card Guard
- ♣ Magma Man
- ♣ Fire Imp

- ♣ Jabberspawn
- ♣ Boojum
- ♣ Phantasmagoria
- ♣ Queen of Hearts—Throne Room (Boss)
- ♣ Queen of Hearts—Netherworld (Boss)

Royal Rage

You didn't think you were done with the mighty Jabberwock, did you? After recovering from Gryphon's extraction of its eye, the Queen's guardian is back and he's really, really peeved.

After the Jabberwock defeats Gryphon in airborne combat, you must finish him off.

Unfortunately the Jabberwock now has the freedom to fly. The monster is many times more dangerous from the air. Your first goal is to keep him on the ground.

The Jabberwock has several attacks:

♣ The fire breath attack is his bread-and-butter weapon. He uses it from the air and on land, while moving and standing still, making the Jabberwock a veritable pyromaniac. The fire breath has a moderate range, but it can be sustained for long stretches of time. The Jabberwock tracks you relentlessly while spitting fire—it's very difficult to avoid being set ablaze.

♣ The beast's physical attacks are fast and indefensible. Claw swipes, stomps, bites tear you apart if you don't constantly stay on the move.

♣ Without both eyes, the Jabberwock can't use his eye beam but he can still fire off the occasional energy burst (the same as you get from the staff when you cease firing). The impact from this blast sends you careening clear out of the arena.

The fire breath is the attack he uses the most.

The eye burst is a one-hit death in this small arena surrounded by a bottomless abyss.

Watch the claws!

Meta-Essence is scarce but can be found in the corners and near Gryphon.

There isn't much Meta-Essence to be had here, so work efficiently and run *a lot*. Crystals appear in the corners of the arena and near Gryphon's body. Unfortunately, they're small and only appear one at a time.

The Jabberwock can't fly if he's severely injured, so try to do as much damage as possible early on.

Start with a Blunderbuss shot.

Immediately arm the Blunderbuss and land a shot in the monster's chest. This exhausts your Strength of Will supply in one fell swoop. Collect a Meta-Essence Crystal and switch to the Eyestaff.

Your most effective weapon is the Eyestaff. Use it until it exhausts your supply of Strength of Will, then search for more Meta-Essence.

Spend the next phase running and dodging. Use the Gryphon's body as cover. Try to keep the Jabberwock in your sights at all times and unload the Eyestaff on him whenever you have Strength of Will to spare.

The Jabberwock is far easier to fight when he's earthbound.

Once sufficiently disabled, the Jabberwock stops flying. This makes him easier to hit, but not easier to fight. His fast, long strides make it nearly impossible to get any distance between you.

Stay on the move and avoid the edges of the arena. Keep firing with the Eyestaff or other weapons until the Jabberwock expires.

When the drawbridge drops, proceed over it and into the Queen of Hearts' realm.

Head under the drawbridge into the Queen's realm.

Battle Royale

Walk the long path up to the base of the Queen's castle.
As you near the first corner, a sole Card Guard is joined by several others.

Feeling a bit outnumbered? Don't worry, the Blunderbuss evens the odds.

Tip

FEEL FREE TO USE YOUR MOST STRENGTH-OF-WILL–DRAINING TOYS. THE META-ESSENCE CRYSTALS YOU GET FROM THE LARGE GANGS OF ENEMIES YOU DESTROY SHOULD BE NUMEROUS ENOUGH TO REFILL EVEN A TOTALLY DRAINED SUPPLY.

Note

DON'T FORGET TO USE THE
DEAD TIME WATCH IN
THIS LEVEL.

Melt the Magma Men.

At the next bend, shatter two Magma
Men. Round a small bend uneventfully.

As you round back toward the castle
wall, groups of Card Guards leap in two
waves from the battlements above.

*The Darkened Looking Glass hides near
a torch by the castle wall.*

At this bend, look for a torch burning
on the hill behind the Card Guards. Look
into a Darkened Looking Glass—invisibility is a real boon in the heat of this battle.

Continue along the pathway. As you
near the castle wall, a huge platoon of
Card Guard pounces in two waves. As you
wind back to the wall, another crowd
blocks your path.

Rage on Alice! The Rage Box can be found near the torch.

Above this bend, look for a torch. Next to it is a Rage Box that should make for some fun against those Card Guards.

As you head away from the wall, two more Heart Card Guards drop into a fighting stance.

Rounding the next bend brings you toward the front gates of the castle. Venture through, the worst is yet to come.

One step closer. The gates ahead get you into the Queen's stronghold.

Ascension

You find yourself on a path far below the Queen's castle on the opposite side of a lava moat. There's no direct way to reach the castle's drawbridge; find a stealthier way in.

The castle itself is high on the hill to your right. You're going to have to take an indirect route.

Jump down and back up.

Walk forward down the path until it abruptly ends. Hop down to a rock in the gap and pull yourself back up to the path.

Move carefully around the support column and pick off two Heart Card Guards. Jump to their position.

Move around the support post to face two Heart Card Guards.

Unless you want a heart bomb in your back, you'll want to get rid of these guys behind you. Your next destination is their sniping post.

As you climb the support, wheel around to slaughter two Heart Card Guards on a high platform.

Pull up on the ledge and jump to the next support.

Pull up on this ledge and leap over to the next support.

Move straight and when you run out of ground, leap to the next support.
Climb up the support toward the castle. At the top, drop down *to the right side.*

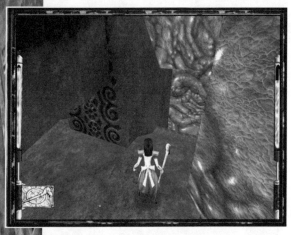

Doesn't look like there's a way in here, but there is.

Secret Passage, Part 1

Look carefully along the wall; a hidden entrance leads to a path inside the cliff.

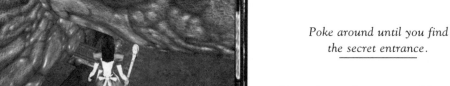

Poke around until you find the secret entrance.

Drop down the steps and head across a long bridge loaded with Card Guards.

Keep your balance and knock the Card Guards off this bony bridge.

After you're safely across the bridge, race through the doorway and up a ramp. Pull up to the high ledge to the right.

Outside Again

As you temporarily leave the secret passage, decapitate the squad of Fire Imps manning the ledges.

Walk to the end of the path and drop down to the path below. After the path ends, turn to pick off a Fire Imp standing on a pylon to the right.

Face the end of the path and jump up to the rocks that block it. Cross the moat via the support and turn left to fight a pair of Fire Imps. Continue forward and enter another secret passage.

The second secret passage.

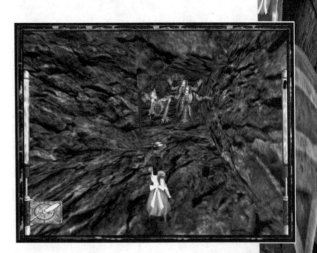

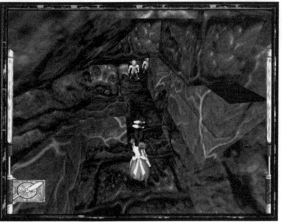

Secret Passage, Part 2

The entrance is guarded by two Boojums and a Jabberspawn.

Continue through the passage into a small opening, and overpower three Fire Imps.

Squeeze through this small hole in the wall.

Climb the wall to the right, but be ready to fight a Phantasmagoria. Ride the steam up and immediately whomp the waiting Heart Card Guard.

This is the first of two steam jets that help you get to the surface. Be ready to fight when you reach the top.

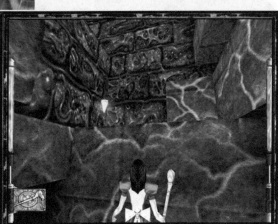

Turn left and drop onto the head of another Heart Card Guard. Trust your fate to the steam jet and ride way up.

Disembark from the steam jet when you reach this height.

When you can rise no farther, float to solid ground. Climb the ledges to return to the relatively fresh air outside.

These ledges lead up and out.

Castle Doors

Use the lower ledges to work your way down to the bridge.

Cross to the ominous castle and eviscerate the two Heart Card Guards manning the doors. Go inside.

So close. Climb carefully down to the bridge and demand entrance to the Queen's castle.

Castle Foyer

Fight your way up the ramp through the legion of Heart and Spade Card Guards. Keep your eyes peeled for Grasshopper Tea and several large Meta-Essence Crystals.

The confines are tight, the enemies numerous, and the battle intense. Why not stop for some Grasshopper Tea?

At the top of the main ramp, descend the ramp on the other side.

Go down the ramp and onto the elevator.
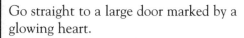

Gut the final Heart Card Guard and make a break for the elevator. Ride it up to the Queen's keep.

Castle Keep

Keep Plaza

Go straight to a large door marked by a glowing heart.

This door leads to the Mirror Gallery and, indirectly, to the Queen's throne room.

Mirror Gallery

After the door opens, contend with three Spade Card Guards (one straight ahead and two others hidden to the right and left).

In the center of this room is a large mirror on a platform. Cross the room via the right or left paths. The large door leads to the Queen's throne room. It's locked. Two Heart Guards defend the door and a switch.

This switch makes the mirror on the platform rotate to the three portraits.

The switch controls the mirror below. Three portraits line the wall around the mirror.

Tweedledee

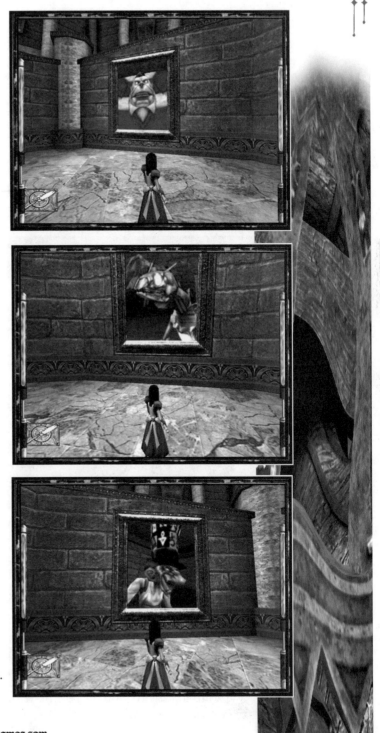

Jabberwock

Mad Hatter

Pull the switch once and the mirror spins to face the Tweedledee portrait. Jump into the submerged area to look at the mirror. Instead of Dee's ugly mug, the mirror displays the image of a Club.

Pulling the switch twice more turns the mirror to face the other two paintings. The secret icons on each painting are:

Tweedledee: Club

Jabberwock: Diamond

Mad Hatter: Spade

Return to the keep plaza.

Plaza Gallery, Again

Walk around the room to either the left or right and obliterate the two Heart Card Guards.

Steam is your elevator to the second floor.

Around the back of the wall, ride the steam jet up to the second floor.

Upper Floor

The horseshoe-shaped hallway of this second floor opens onto three doors. Each door is marked with a symbol:

Diamond Room, right.

Club Room, middle.

Spade Room, left.

Each door is unlocked by pointing the mirror at one of the paintings in the Mirror Gallery. Orienting the mirror, therefore, has the following effects:

Portrait	Opens Room
Tweedledee	Club
Jabberwock	Diamond
Mad Hatter	Spade

Orient the mirror toward the Tweedledee portrait and return to the Club Room.

Club Room

Trudge down the dark bridge. When you reach the end of the walkway, the lights come on and the three portraits appear in the air above.

Throw your Vorpal Blade to select Tweedledee.

Throw your Vorpal Blade at the Tweedledee portrait.

One of the three locks to the Queen's Throne Room is now unlocked.

Return to the Mirror Gallery and pull the switch to orient the mirror to the Jabberwock portrait, then go to the Diamond Room.

Diamond Room

Go to the end of the walkway and throw your Blade at the portrait of the Jabberwock.

Here, it's the Jabberwock.

The second of three locks is now undone.

Adjust the mirror in the Mirror Gallery to face the Mad Hatter portrait and head straight to the Spade Room.

Spade Room

Throw your Blade at the Mad Hatter portrait.

And here, it's the Mad Hatter.

The final lock is now released.

Note

THROWING YOUR BLADE AT THE INCORRECT PORTRAIT AUTOMATICALLY TRANSPORTS YOU BACK TO THE MIRROR ROOM TO FACE TWO NEW SPADE GUARDS. MOVE QUICKLY OUT OF THE CROSSFIRE. YOU'LL NEED TO PULL THE SWITCH THREE TIMES TO BRING THE MIRROR BACK TO THE CORRECT PORTRAIT. THEN, RETURN TO THE APPROPRIATE ROOM AND TARGET THE CORRECT PAINTING.

The door in the Mirror Room is now open.

Return to the Mirror Gallery after fighting two Heart Card Guards who've taken up positions in the keep plaza.

Mirror Gallery, Again

Pass through the now-open door to the throne room atrium.

Throne Room Atrium

Cross the bridge over the pool of blood to the door leading to the Queen's throne room.

Heart of Darkness

You've finally come face to face with the dreaded Queen herself. Like the rest of Wonderland, she's not as you remember her.

The battle begins immediately. The Queen is moored to her throne by a long, repulsive tentacle. Just because she can't move far, however, doesn't mean she can't get to you whenever she wants—her powers extend way beyond her physical reach.

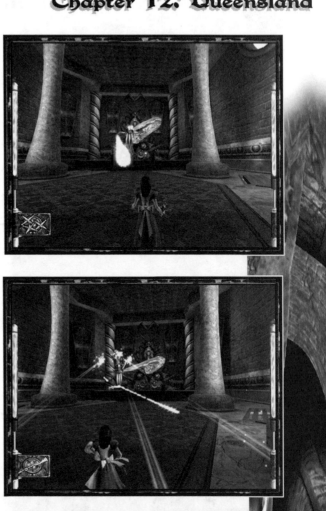

This snowball stings a lot. Luckily it's easy to avoid.

Tentacles spread wide means there are either missiles or energy beams coming at you.

When you see light form around you, move forward or backward quickly!

Once you're brought in for a hug, there's no escape.

Note

ALMOST ALL OF THE QUEEN'S ATTACKS HAVE DISTINCTIVE SOUNDS ASSOCIATED WHEN THEM. ONCE YOU LEARN TO RECOGNIZE THESE, YOU WON'T EVEN NEED TO SEE THE QUEEN TO KNOW WHAT'S COMING.

After you see a tentacle plunge into the ground, you have only a second to move out of the way before it comes back up.

♣ The Queen spreads her arms and a cloud of blue or yellow light forms around you. In a moment, you'll be either slammed against the wall or brought in for a big, nasty hug. To avoid both fates, run forward or backward as the light begins to form around you. You have only an instant to get out of harm's way. Learn to recognize the attack even before the cloud starts forming.

♣ She stabs her tentacle into the floor and it almost instantly rises from the floor wherever you're standing. Sidestep in the instant before the tentacle arrives to avoid it.

♣ When she extends all of her tentacles, she fires either energy beams (hard to avoid) or "rockets" (easier to avoid) or both. Strafing and taking cover behind columns provide adequate protection.

♣ The snowball freezes you solid for a moment. When you see the Queen join her hands together to form a ball of white light, wait for her to launch the snowball and sidestep this slow-moving projectile.

You're not entirely safe back here, but you're shielded from projectile attacks.

Use the pillars for cover from frontal assaults, but beware the tentacle and wall slam that can get you even when you're not in the Queen's line of sight.

Refuel with Meta-Essence Crystals whenever you can.

Unlike many other battles, there's no trick to fighting the Queen. It's a straightforward battle with lots of clever defense. Your main concerns are avoiding and countering the Queen's attacks, then peck away at her as frequently as possible.

The Blunderbuss is very effective, but uses considerable Strength of Will.

No single weapon is preferable, though you won't be able to get close enough to use any melee weapons. Particularly effective are the Blunderbuss and the Eyestaff. The Ice Wand is good for defense (the ice shield), and the Jacks do considerable damage.

Playin' possum. Don't give up just because she looks spent. You'll know when it's over.

The Queen likes to play dead, hanging listlessly from her tentacle before launching a quick attack. Whenever you think you've beaten her, keep firing away until there's no doubt.

Though you've won the first battle, she isn't finished with you. The Queen drags you to a final battle with her true, inner self.

Demon Queen

This arena is a circle of rock islands. The ones at the corners are larger, providing safer fighting ground.

There's plenty of jumping to do in this floating arena.

The Queen floats in the center of the ring; she can change position but only by diving down into the darkness and resurfacing elsewhere.

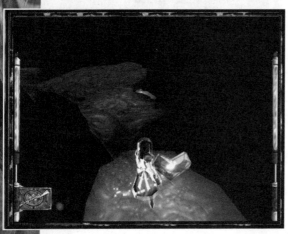

Be on the lookout for these huge Meta-Essence Crystals.

Large Meta-Essence Crystals appear on the smaller islands periodically. Only one appears at a time.

The demonic incarnation of the Queen is a more powerful and straightforward opponent than the version you've already beaten.

The belly scream can knock you off ledges or out of jumps.

The gas attack has remarkable distance.

The missiles hurt and infect you with Spider venom.

♣ The gaping hole in her belly serves several functions. First, it fires projectiles from long distances.

♣ Second, the Queen emits a disruptive scream from her belly. Like the Boojum scream, it inflicts damage as it knocks you back and, potentially, off the platforms.

♣ From her left side, she fires a splatter of green liquid that scorches flesh, which is easy to avoid by sidestepping.

♣ She also fires the same missiles as the Mad Hatter. These are tipped with Nightmare Spider venom and cause the same temporary disorientation and partial blindness.

♣ She often dives below your view and resurfaces directly in front of you. Take a new position while she's out of sight and you might get a clean shot while she's facing the other direction.

♣ When she gets in close, she swipes at you with her tentacles.

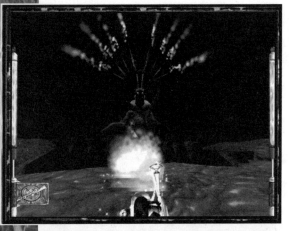

Start by waiting for the Queen to dive out of sight. When she reemerges, let her have it with a Blunderbuss shot or a hit with the Eyestaff.

Hit her with the Blunderbuss right off the bat.

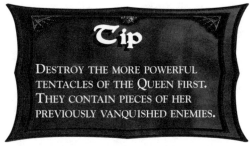

Tip

DESTROY THE MORE POWERFUL TENTACLES OF THE QUEEN FIRST. THEY CONTAIN PIECES OF HER PREVIOUSLY VANQUISHED ENEMIES.

Turn right and leap to the big Meta-Essence Crystal. Continue jumping until you get to the large corner platform.

Look below for the Blunderbuss, even if you already have the weapon.

Turn around and look down for a white-lit ledge. Drop to it. If you don't already have the Blunderbuss, here's your chance. If you do have it, good news: Taking it refills your Strength of Will.

Step onto the square near this ledge to transport yourself back up to the corner platform.

Fire away and reload to fire again.

Fire the Blunderbuss right into the Queen's belly.
Jump around the ring to collect two more large Meta-Essence Crystals to regain full Strength of Will. Fire again!
The pattern from here on out is fire, get two crystals, and repeat.

You'll be certain when this Queen is dead.

When the Queen begins to convulse and her "crown" falls from her head, you can be assured of your victory.
Wonderland and young Alice's Sanity are restored. It's as if it was all a wonderfully horrible dream.

part III
Cheats
&
Interview

Cheats

For those times when playing fair just doesn't get the job done, there are some cheats available to help you out in *American McGee's Alice*, though there's a cost for using them.*

These cheats are entered via the console. First, make sure the console is enabled in the Game Options section of the Settings menu.

To open the console, press ~.

When the console drops down, input your desired cheat and press Return. Then, press ~ again to put the console away.

Type in the cheats exactly as they appear in the table column titled "Console Command." The cheats available in *American McGee's Alice* are:

Cheat Name	What It Does	Console Command
God Mode	Alice is invulnerable; Toys don't consume Strength of Will	god
No Clip Mode	Alice can move through walls and fly; she can't attack	noclip
No Target Mode	Enemies take no notice of Alice	notarget
All Toys Mode	Grants Alice all Toys and refills Sanity and Strength of Will	give all

*Note that these cheats will suck much of the fun right out of the game. Use them at your own discretion, but don't blame us if you feel all empty inside. All players, including those who recognize these cheats from other games, should realize that employing them may have unpredictable results. They are designed as diagnostic tools, not as gameplay - assistance.

Interview with American McGee

Q: Tell me about your background. Where were you raised and educated? What inspired you to begin designing and what drew you to the gaming industry?

A: Background, hmmm … born and raised in Dallas, Texas. Never finished high school. Had a pretty "interesting" childhood to say the least. Was brought into the games industry through one of those "right place right time" scenarios. Strongly believe that everything happens for a reason and that all the events leading up to my being here today have an influence on one another and my creations.

Q: Why did you choose *Alice*? What about the book said to you "decapitating Card Guards"?

A: I choose *Alice* because the characters and environments really spoke to me. In them I saw the chance to do something unique in a game, and to really expand the current genre.

What said "decapitating card guards"? I believe it was the Queen of Hearts. Making this version of *Alice* wasn't much of a stretch from the original fiction. In comparison, I think the Disney version is further away from the original than *Alice* ended up.

Q: Do you believe that the Alice books are really "children's books?"

A: Technically, no. But that's not to say that I would withhold that book (or any work of literature for that matter) from the hands of a child. Regardless, the Alice books may have been written for and about a child, but at the same time they contained commentary on politics that I doubt any child would comprehend or enjoy. Part of the beauty of the writing is that it can simultaneously serve two very different functions, and do both well.

Q: There seem to be several influences at work in the game's visual aesthetic. Is there anything you were consciously drawing on when creating the game's look? To what extent did you feel constrained by the books' well-known John Tenniel artistic renderings?

A: My personal aesthetic as well as that of the Rogue team influenced the game. At the end of the day, my own contributions were mostly influenced by my appreciation of certain styles of art, fashion, music, and gameplay. Not once did I feel constrained by the art or original fiction, to the contrary, I felt an obligation to maintain a high level of creativity and artistic credibility. It was a challenge to live up to what we were basing the game on.

Q: Perception and perspective seem to be recurrent themes in the design of the game's levels. Is there a guiding theme that you wanted to communicate to the player?

A: There is certainly a guiding theme, and it's woven in to many elements of the world, characters, and story. Once you get into the game and the fiction, you'll start to identify it, and hopefully by the end of the game you'll suddenly have that "aha!" moment where you realize what it was all about.

Q: This game proudly bears your very distinctive name. To what extent is this a signature "American McGee" game? Is *Alice* a realization of your distinctive, individual vision or is it a collaborative effort like most games?

A: *Alice* was very much a collaborative effort between Rogue Entertainment, EA, and me. Without the Rogue team's amazing creative input and hard work, *Alice* would have never seen the light of day. On the EA side, our producer R.J. Berg, an army of marketing, PR, and others saw to it that everything went smoothly and that Rogue had all the support that they needed to make Alice happen. As for it being a "signature game," I'm both proud and embarrassed to have my name on the box. Embarrassed because so many other people contributed to making *Alice* so amazing. Proud because it's wonderful to have my name so closely tied to such amazing work.

Q: Was *Alice* something you've wanted to do for some time or did it come to you while working on another project?

A: It came to me about a year before we actually started work on it. It was inspired by a number of things, including a group of friends, a song, and a frustration with the current offering of games.

Q: Is there an American McGee design style? Is there, in other words, an earmark that reveals your imagination?

A: Not really. At least not one that I'm aware of. I'd like to think that I'm original, not predictable, and certainly not analyzable on the basis of a single "earmark."

Q: Speculate on what Lewis Carroll would think of *American McGee's Alice*?

A: First, he would probably freak and run out of the room. Once someone managed to explain to him that computers weren't the work of Satan … imagine he might be pleased. I've heard it said many times now that our Wonderland is closer to people's visions of the original than anything that's been created before.

Q: If, in high school, someone had told you what you'd be doing at this point in your life, how would you have reacted?

A: Most likely I would have been angry with them for telling me how my life was going to turn out. I prefer to learn that kind of stuff in real time and to live my life in the moment. Knowing your future takes all the fun out of getting there.

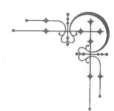